CLASSROOM OBSERVATION

A GUIDE TO

CLASSROOM OBSERVATION

Rob Walker
Clem Adelman

Photographs by Janine Wiedel

Methuen and Co Ltd

First published 1975 by Methuen & Co Ltd
11 New Fetter Lane London EC4P 4EE

© 1975 Rob Walker and Clem Adelman

Typeset by Preface Ltd, Salisbury
Printed in Great Britain by
Butler & Tanner Ltd, Frome and London

ISBN (hardbound) 0 416 812 00 7
ISBN (paperback) 0 416 81210 4

Distributed in the USA by
HARPER & ROW PUBLISHERS INC.
BARNES & NOBLE IMPORT DIVISION

Contents

Acknowledgements

Our thanks:

To the teachers who participated in our study groups at the Centre for Science Education 1971–2 and 1972–3. Because of them the ideas in this book emerged in the way they did.

To Jim Binham, Colin Muge, Ann Hall, Martin Phillipson, Neville Jones, Berris Bowen, Lezli Weintrobe and Miriam Smith-Philipson for allowing us to observe and record in their classes and to use extracts and photographs in this book. To Tony Malpas for first suggesting we write the book.

To Ann Fiander for the quotation from her dissertation.

To Cyril Daltry and Margaret Brown for the quotations from mathematics students.

To Harold Silver, whose imagination and commitment to teacher education made it possible. Few researchers can have had the opportunities to realize their ideas in the way we did.

To Chelsea College, the SSRC, the Central Research Fund of the University of London and the Ford Foundation for their financial support at various times since 1968.

To Basil Bernstein.

To John Elliott and Barry MacDonald.

To George Gross

To Alan and Diana Fone.

To Pat Clipsham, electric typist.

To Liz, Lynne, Ben and Tomsk.

The authors and publishers would also like to thank the following for permission to reproduce material from the publications cited:

The *Daily Express* for the cartoon by Giles; the *Daily Telegraph* for the quotation from their issue of 13 December 1973; the *Guardian* for the cartoon by Horner; Hutchinson & Co Ltd for M. L. J. Abercrombie, *Anatomy of Judgement*; John Wiley and Sons Ltd for Willard Waller, *The Sociology of Teaching*; Penguin Books Ltd for Douglas Barnes, James Britton, and Harold Rosen, *Language, the Learner and the School*; Random House for Immanuel Wallerstein and Paul Starr, *The University Crisis Reader*, Vol. I, and Jules Henry, *Culture Against Man*; Simon and Schuster Inc and Deborah Rogers Ltd for Sylvia Ashton-Warner, *Teacher* (© 1963, Sylvia Ashton-Warner); the Editor of *Visual Education* and the author for Robert Jardine, 'An exploration in the use of videotape recording in teacher–pupil relationships' (The National Council for Audio-visual Aids in Education). Cyrilly Abels for permission to reprint part of *The Totalitarian Classroom: A Learning Game*, © 1969 Michael Rossman.

The Observation Handbook:
a guide for students on first teaching practice.

QUESTIONS ASKED BY MATHEMATICS STUDENTS BEFORE THEIR FIRST TEACHING PRACTICE

When should punishment be used and what is an effective and permissible form of punishment?

How should one cope with individual personality clashes or the attention-seeking pupil?

How should one cope with external disruptions to class such as medical visits?

How to cope with mixed ability problems?

How to cope with language problems? Nationality or region, or speech difficulty or obscene language.

What is the best way of supervising equipment?

How often to prepare *homework* — and how much to give them — what should homework consist of?

How should one group the class — by friends, by ability, randomly?

How should one deal with personal comments about staff?

How to cope with crushes?

What should be your attitude over copying? How does one deal with copying, e.g. homework?

What to do in case of illness/accident?

How to cope and keep control with your back to the class?

What to do if a child misses essential work through illness and is a long way behind the others?

What to do if a number of the children refuse to do anything you tell them?

What to wear?

How to deal with children seen misbehaving outside school?

Relationships with other staff members?

Who is legally responsible for the class while we are on teaching practice?

How do you start with a new class?

How can you discipline people who e.g. throw paper aeroplanes, are cheeky?

What do you do if you cannot answer a question?

How do you regain control of a class?

How do you learn their names — surnames or first names? How do you address those whose names you don't know?

What do you do if someone doesn't want to learn?

What do you do when you are physically threatened by a pupil?

How does one deal with an irate parent?

What do you do if a fight breaks out in your class?

What does one do about direct questions about morals, ethics?

How much does one follow the head's opinion, directions? Is it a rat race?

How does a teacher act if he (she) feels a child is suffering at home, e.g. beatings, neglect?

How severely do you keep discipline?

What do you do if you are left in charge of a class without having prepared a lesson?

What happens if the children say they are bored by the lesson?

COMMENTS MADE BY MATHEMATICS STUDENTS ON THEIR PRELIMINARY PRACTICE

I was struck by:

the wide variation in standards of attainment in any class.

the way enthusiasm communicated itself from some teachers.

chaos . . .

how well-behaved the children were.

(the fact that) although they could do the working the children weren't sure what fractions and decimals *were*.

how many children were really lost.

(the fact that) children couldn't visualize areas, sizes of.

the range of intelligence.

the frustration and lack of idealism among teachers.

the girls (being) . . . much keener workers.

(the fact that) there were forty-three in my class and the backward ones were . . .

how the slow children appreciated what you did for them.

(the fact that) the masters had a friendly atmosphere in their classes, but when I took over . . .

(the fact that) every lesson seemed to be a lesson in English.

(the fact that) the children were disciplined but they weren't understanding.

(the fact that) the children went out to measure the football field — even so they could still talk of 'square acres'.

the range of intelligence — how do you cope?

how helpful they were (the children) to me, a student teacher.

the complications of giving out pencils and equipment.

the use by infants of Cuisenaire (rods).

children's capacity to help themselves.

(the fact that) these juniors liked having someone there all the time (staff shortage).

(the fact that) the (girls') school was keen on trying new experiments, but it was bluff.

how the children forgot from week to week.

(the fact that) in my school they seemed to have no real difficulty at all.

(the fact that) though children couldn't do written work they were devastatingly keen observers, e.g. details in acting, miming.

(the fact that) the children weren't keen to progress in arithmetic.

(this thought) think at level of slower children!

how the teachers' personalities were reflected in the way they gave their lessons.

the surprising advance juniors make in one year.

the misery of a secondary modern school in the Midlands with an immigrant population. The children couldn't understand the teachers' speech.

the variations in children's capacity.

(this thought) there was an unstreamed school, one boy ESN but parents refused to allow him to go to a special school: he needed a lot of time.

the complicated patterns of streaming.

the marking and position lists . . .

"Yes, I did hear how the lady in Mr. Warhol's film did her painting, but we in Class 2 are sticking to the old-fashioned brush method."

Observation soon reveals the classroom as a complex social system

(*Daily Express* 18 January 1973.)

Going on teaching practice — observation

Most initial courses for teachers adopt a plan for easing students into teaching by allowing them to observe experienced teachers at work. Colleges vary considerably in the way they organize and prepare for this period of initial observation. Some primary courses direct observation to particular aspects of child development by extensive lecture and seminar sessions, and then control observation periods, gradually building up from half-day sessions to longer periods. In other colleges students may find themselves in a school for periods of several weeks armed only with an initial reading list and a satisfactory X-ray certificate.

The schools, too, vary in the way they receive students. Students may arrive fresh from the college expecting to spend several days 'observing', only to be told, 'I'm afraid we're very short-staffed this week. Would you mind sitting in with 2B this lesson? They've got the work to do, so you shouldn't have any problems.' The students who survives 2B is likely to graduate rapidly to 4H, and may feel at the end of a week that this baptism of fire has taught him far more than he would have learnt sitting meekly at the sidelines watching a master teacher at work.

If observation is taken to mean simply sitting and watching, the observational period is usually one of unease, a transitional state between being student and being teacher. Few students seem to know quite what to look for, or how to learn from the experience; they often become bored. Teachers can feel anxious having someone watching them teach and are happy to move the student into a more active phase. In classes where the teacher is more informal the transition is easier and smoother and the observational role presents fewer problems.

In what follows we have tried to set out an approach to observation which takes into account the variations and discontinuities that exist between courses, between schools and between classrooms. In what we propose we hope that the primary and secondary school student teachers, however prepared, and whatever the nature of the school setting they enter, will be able to find something helpful and useful.

Originally we wrote these observation notes as a guide to teaching practice for *students*. What we found from trying the notes out in a number of colleges and university departments was that there was just as much need for the guide among college tutors and supervising teachers in schools as there was among students themselves. This book is aimed at both student teachers *and* at those responsible for their supervision; for while their problems are different their concerns are very similar. What we hope most of all is that these books will provide a means by which students and supervisors can communicate with each other. The basis of their relationship, which is the collision of theory and experience, is critical for education and underlies all we have written.

Being an observer

Being an observer is a transitional role, and the time spent in it will be different for different students. What they are expected to get out of it will also vary, as will the extent and kind of documentation their college tutors will want them to produce. We want to develop the idea that the observational role is not simply a temporary role that the student leaves behind, but that it is a role that he or she internalizes and carries on into their teaching. We believe that good teachers are those who are able, at critical points, to distance themselves from classroom activities, to see themselves as others see them, and to adjust their actions accordingly.

In this book we aim to approach this ideal by doing two things. One is to try and make the period of observation

What you see in a school will depend on how the school sees you

As a new face in the school you are likely to be observed as closely as you will be observing. One of the first things you will have to adjust to is being looked at. Just what questions lie behind the eyes that watch you is something you will have to learn to ascertain.

interesting. Students often complain that they find observation boring, and one of the things we have tried to do is to suggest things to look for, and to imply ways of looking at them that will make the period of observation interesting. This is what the 'Observation handbook' tries to do. It is not intended to be a programmed workbook, but to offer starting points. Essentially it is about research, for it is about how to begin discovering about your own situation, about how to create data that can form the basis for taking action.

The second part of the book, which we have called the 'Observation resource book', is complementary to the first, and is about how to get from the data back to action. It tries to provide ways for students to carry the information generated by the 'Observation handbook' back into the classroom in a way that they can use to adapt their own teaching. The idea underlying both parts of the book is that it is necessary to create a cycle between perception and action. That it is not enough simply to go into a classroom and come out with lucid descriptions or crisp analyses. Ways have to be found of taking these ideas back into the classroom so as to form the basis for further observations. What we are working towards is teachers becoming their own researchers and evaluators.

It follows that we do *not* see observation as a discrete, transitional role between learning and teaching; we *do* see it as an important, integral element of *both* learning and teaching.

Many people talk about observation as though it were natural social behaviour which everyone included in their repertoire of social skills. In some ways perhaps this is true, but it is also true that for a student to be placed in a classroom as an observer is a novel experience, and one which he or she has to learn to cope with, for in some ways students know too much about classrooms, having spent many thousands of hours in them as both pupils and students. What they know about classrooms is biased, a partial view of what really goes on.

The essential problem of observation at this stage is to *unlearn* the pupil perspective in order to manage the transition to teacher. (We are careful to use the word 'unlearn' and not 'forget'.) The teacher sees the class quite differently from the way it is seen by the child. Children are faced with the problem of either producing a performance that the teacher requires, or reacting against it in some way. In either event, a major element in the classroom situation fo the pupils is what they take to be the demands of the teache: whether these are stated or unstated. For them the situation is inevitably one of constraint, and initially one of their main concerns will be to test out the precise nature of the demands that are being made on them in order to find out how much freedom of action they have in carrying out what the teacher seems to be demanding.

For the teacher the problem is quite different: his task is to get beyond the constraints as rapidly as possible; he has to define the situation and set the pace — to make sure that what he wants to happen seems to happen.

For many people starting teaching, it comes as a shock to realize that the spotlight is on them, that the initiative is in their hands, that they suddenly have responsibility for what happens, what will happen and what might happen. The classroom, which they saw previously as an unshakeable social structure, suddenly becomes bewildering and problematic, fraught with difficulties at every turn. Many consequently exaggerate in their minds the degree to which the situation is 'out of control' simply because they are unaware of the change in perspective brought about by the shift from the back to the front of the class. Most children have a limited notion of the consequences their actions have for the classroom as a continuing social situation, but teachers are put in a position where they are made highly aware of the effects, intended and unintended, that their actions can have on the situation. This realization can be a shock to many beginning teachers. They suddenly see the classroom through different eyes.

In some vague way the period of observation is fitted into courses of initial training to help the student manage this dramatic change in roles, but in many ways the ideal role for an observer is the converse of that of the successful teacher; the ideal observer tends to be unobtrusive, static and as far as possible outside the inclusive classroom group. The observer is outside the action looking in, a non-reactive presence taking the role of audience rather than performer.

This is not to say that teachers do not find, or even create, spaces for themselves in the course of normal lessons, where they can temporarily take on the role of observer. But these moments of contemplation, in which a participant stands back from the stream of classroom activity, are necessarily fragmented, brief and easily disturbed.

This is one reason why we want to stress that for teachers the observational role is not important in itself, but is only useful for the kind of information it makes it possible to collect about what is going on in the classroom. The observer can see things that teachers cannot see, and can use this information to make himself a better teacher.

Becoming an observer: some guidelines

Whether you are a student on teaching practice, a college supervisor or a research worker, whether you are young or old, male or female, who you appear to be to the inhabitants of the school will influence their response to your presence and the kind of image of themselves and their situation that they share with you. What you see in a school as an observer is partly a function of how the school sees you. The observer's view, like the participant's, is always partial. Observers who think they have access to the springs of objective knowledge, who feel themselves to be the only people who know the 'truth', are likely to be on shaky ground. This ground rule of observational research has important implications which will be different for the researcher, the supervisor and the teacher.

With familiarity, *who* you are in the school becomes a matter of personal rather than social identity. People react to you as the person they feel you to be, rather than to your status as supervisor, student, researcher etc. It is still true that however well teachers and children know you, and however careful you are, your presence will have some effect on what happens and on how people act. Initially your presence will create ripples generated by your official status, but as you become known the ripples will be caused by your actions as the person you are perceived to be.

This is important because most people are able to detect reactions to their presence that stem from their social identity and status. There is in such reactions a feeling of lack of fit between the person you feel yourself to be and the way in which people seem to be responding to you — a feeling that 'it will be easier when we know each other'. What most people find more difficult is to develop some awareness of responses to themselves as persons. Naturally the tendency is simply to respond and not to be aware of the qualities of the transaction. It is, for example, quite easy in an established relationship to find yourself expressing and feeling anger without really knowing how the situation arose. Simply knowing that the incident itself seems trivial only makes things worse; you have to learn to admit your feelings and then to monitor the patterns of actions and feelings that create such situations.

When we talk about 'observation', we do not simply mean watching and describing what seems to be going on in a classroom: we want to include attempts to reconcile ourselves to our own feelings and responses to events. Admitting to ourselves that we get angry or frustrated, that we like or dislike other teachers or particular children, are the kinds of things we have to come to terms with as teachers. The 'observational role' as we want to try and develop it is one step in this direction.

Some degree of sensitivity to the way in which different situations respond to your presence as an observer can also be used as a key to open up the underlying structure of the situations themselves. With experience you can begin to recognize some of the influences your presence has on both teachers in different schools and different classes. Classes where your presence makes a big impact are usually different kinds of classes from those where you feel invisible. This variation may be due to differences in schools, in subjects, in classes, in teachers, in the architecture, in your own behaviour. Practice and experience give you patterns of expectation and a repertoire of corresponding actions.

In everyday life we all adjust our actions in many subtle ways to different settings and situations. There are many possible ways of varying how we dress, how we sit and stand, how close we get to the people we talk to, the level and rhythm of our speech, as well as what we actually say. According to where we are, and the age, sex and status of others present, we modify the way in which we present ourselves to others. These mechanisms of adjustment we often recognize in others, but not in ourselves. For example, many people have a 'telephone voice' that they use only when talking to people on the phone, but it takes an outside observer to be aware of this particular style of talking — it is not something we generally recognize in ourselves. But for the serious observer of social life, whether in classrooms or in other settings, sensitivity to our own behaviour can tell us

something of the setting and situation we are in. We can use ourselves as instruments to detect and amplify differences between situations that superficially might seem very similar.

With this in mind we can make some specific recommendations about observing in classrooms.

1. PLACING YOURSELF IN THE ROOM

Generally you want to be in a position where you can observe most but intrude least in the activities of the class. In a traditional classroom where all desks face the front, the usual place to put the observer is somewhere at the back. This means you can watch the teacher from afar without distracting the pupils too much, but it also means that you cannot see their faces. The view of the lesson you tend to get is therefore a kind of reflection of the image that the teacher has — you see the lesson in the teacher's mind's eye, taught to a mass of anonymous faces. If you have to sit at the back, try and sit to one side so that you can at least see something of the children's faces — watching them can often tell you more about what is happening than watching the teacher.

Ideally you should be able to take in the whole room with a short eye-scan, yet be close enough to at least one group to be able to listen in to their conversations reasonably unobtrusively. During any kind of classwork or practical activity the talk of a work group can tell you a good deal about the way in which the group organizes itself and goes about the task.

It is important to avoid coming between people who might want to communicate with each other, or to block access to important resources. (One researcher told us that he visited a school and was observing a lesson but was surprised at the response of the class to his presence. Children kept asking him for things, and he felt that he was somehow in the way. It was only after twenty minutes or so that he realized he was sitting in the teacher's chair.)

2. EYE CONTACT

Eye contact is surprisingly significant in classroom situations. In formal, 'whole-class' teaching, students sometimes find it hard to know where to look — for looking is not simply a means of seeing, but also a communicative action. (See cartoon.)

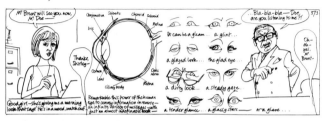

As an observer it is easy to find yourself 'playing teacher', scanning the class and 'fielding' all the glances that pupils throw your way. By returning glances and 'staring out' pupils the observer can often establish a public image of himself as someone who 'knows what is going on', or 'has eyes in the back of his head'. For a student observing a class that he or she will later teach, a lesson spent looking only at the teacher or gazing out of the window might be creating difficulties for the future. For the lesson may be used as an opportunity to establish yourself as someone with what the American psychologist Jacob Kounin* calls 'with-it-ness' — the ability to communicate to the children that you are a person who 'knows what is going on'. On a small scale, this illustrates what we said before about the difference between pupil and teacher perceptions of lessons, and the difficulties of transferring from one perspective to the other.

For most observational purposes it is perhaps best to accept pupil glance without staring back. To either avoid all eye contact, or to 'field' it all, makes you an object of curiosity and highly intrusive. With experience you can begin

*Kounin 1970.

to distinguish those glances that are simply looking you over (and do not require reciprocation) from those which are seeking reciprocal contact. Judging how to respond depends on the kinds of relationship you want to create.

3. DRESS AND PERSONAL STYLE

Dress seems to present more problems in the school as a whole than it does in the classroom. Some headmasters refuse to admit student teachers to their schools because their skirts are too long or too short, or because their hair is too long. In terms of classroom relationships there are distinct problems in being too untidily dressed in poorer areas — it may be perceived by the children as a veiled insult. What the teacher intends as 'being casual' may be interpreted by the children as a form of rejection.

For the researcher who wants to be able to talk to children as well as to teachers, clothing presents additional difficulties. However he dresses he is likely to be seen as aligned more or less strongly with either teachers or kids. The only way out is to contrive some sort of paradox — white shirt and dark suit with an open neck and long hair or, if he can afford it, to dress very fashionably but immaculately, like a football star. Student teachers have the additional problem of whether to dress as a novice teacher or as a temporary observer to the school.

Judging the right personal style is a more difficult thing to manage. We always suggest that students should try to hold back from judging situations publicly, but remain as neutral as is reasonable in the situation. This does not mean remaining uninvolved but means taking the stance recommended by the anthropologist Alan Beals: not disguising or hiding your values, but moderating the level of their expression: 'The dispassionate observer cannot exist since such an observer distorts the data by behaving in an unhuman manner. The solution would seem to be to participate, but to try to limit one's passion and involvement to the minimum expected by the community' (Spindler 1970, p. 33).

Even from observing empty spaces you can learn to read what activities might be appropriate.

Many students enter teaching with strong moral and political beliefs which are so close to their ideas of self that they find it difficult to distance themselves from them. We have known students who have been unable to tolerate the value systems of public schools, and others who have been unhappy in comprehensives. It is difficult for those of us who have taught for some years to appreciate what an involving experience teaching practice can be for a student. We have always tried to get students to see it as a period for 'fieldwork', a period for gathering data about themselves in a novel set of situations. Only occasionally have we succeeded, but we think the aim is still a worthwhile one to pursue. The important thing is to try to free students from a sense of personal failure — to create a context for learning how to teach within which they are free to fail, but within which this failure is not cumulative and can be used creatively.

In the classroom — observation points

These points do not constitute a comprehensive checklist, but are intended to release data for observation. They are also here to help you extend what you see into some sort of context.

A. PHYSICAL SETTING

1. Location of classroom in the building. Is it difficult to find? Is it central or peripheral? How is it related to other nearby rooms? (Is it one of a suite of specialist rooms, or is it isolated?) If corridors — how are they used?

2. Age of buildings. Are all the school buildings the same age?

3. Outlook. Is the room overlooked by other parts of the school? Does it look out to the outside world?

4. Storage of equipment etc. Is it open-access or stored offstage? Location of prep rooms etc. relative to labs.

5. Where are the nearest water taps and sinks? Where are the nearest lavatories — for boys, girls, staff?

6. Where are the emergency exits in case of fire etc.?

7. Degree of specialization in classrooms. How are they identified? (By subject, location code . . .?) If by subject, how specialized are they? Are there 'science labs' or labs for chemistry, physics and biology? Are rooms specialized by the age of children using them (e.g. junior/senior chemistry labs)?

8. Note patterns of wear and tear on furniture and equipment. Broken power points, light fittings, cracked sinks, damaged stools, chairs or desk tops. Patterns of wear on floor tiles can reveal the stability of furniture layout, the quality of pupil movements and bottlenecks in the distribution of resources.

9. Note any unexpected apparatus or equipment — a piano in a physics lab, powder paint in English or chemistry, or noticeably expensive or unusual items like video-tape recorders. Follow these up with teachers and children, find out where they came from, who uses them and how frequently.

10. Note any posters, pictures, wall charts or exhibits, animals or plants. How long have they been there? Do the children notice them? Those that require maintenance (animals etc.) — who looks after them? How is their care organized?

11. Note overall room shape and size and the location of fixed furniture and service points. These can be vital in determining patterns of friendship grouping and informal communication.

12. Location of blackboard, OHP (overhead projector) etc. Is blackboard/screen in a position where everyone can see it? If there is a demonstration bench for science, is its height

such that the class can look down on it?

13. Acoustics of the room. Echo, resonance, ambient noise, aircraft, traffic etc. Can you hear school bell/tannoy? Is the furniture noisy?

14. Temperature, humidity, changing air.

15. Lighting, glare, direct sunlight.

Documentation

1. In some lessons there are quite highly defined territories. The teacher tends to remain within one space (around his desk and the blackboard), the pupils in another. Sometimes it is useful to sketch territory maps for the teacher and for groups of children, remembering you may need several such maps during the course of a lesson.

2. It is useful to compile a list of all the spaces in the school, their official labels and their usual use. Start with a list of the formal teaching spaces as indicated on the timetable, then add others as these seem significant (corridors, houserooms, halls, cloakrooms etc.). In a large school this may be a considerable task — in which case try sampling one block or area.

3. Keep a sharp eye open for discrepancies between the official designation of rooms and spaces and their actual use, e.g. the 'resource centre' that is really a library, the 'language lab' used for ordinary lessons, the 'medical room' used for remedial reading, corridors used for 'project work' . . .

B. PUPILS

1. How many? How old are they? Boys, girls or mixed? Ability? Course? Name/number of class?

2. Notice who arrives first. Do pupils remain in the same groups inside the classroom as those in which they arrived?

3. Look at the overall pattern of spacing between groups of children. Is the spacing uniform, does it reflect the location of furniture/resources or is it related to friendship groups?

4. Estimate the kind and degree of movement within and between groups and the ways in which these change during the course of the lesson.

5. Who are the isolate children?

6. Who is the joker?

7. Which children always raise their hands when the teacher asks a question?

8. Which children never raise their hands to answer a question? (Are they ever asked to respond by the teacher?)

9. Notice the children who sit at the back and in the corners. Is their behaviour any different from that of rest of the class?

10. Who asks for pens, rubbers etc.? Whom do they ask?

11. Try and assess the extent of division of labour within groups. Does each child do much the same as another in carrying out the tasks, or are there different roles? (In science perhaps one takes notes, one takes readings and a third is the experimental subject.) Are the roles fixed, or do children move from one to another? Is there any negotiation over allocation of roles or over who does what? How does the division of labour relate to the way children talk to each other? Are all groups equally cohesive and smooth-running?

12. Is there much communication between groups? Are they aware of what the others are doing? If one group discovers a novel way of doing things, how does this diffuse through the class?

13. When the teacher asks a child a question does it ever get answered by another child in the same friendship group? Is the relationship between the children predominantly protective or competitive?

14. How far do individual children possess territory in the classroom — i.e. do they have areas where other children do not invade?

14

C. TEACHERS

1. How do they enter the room, and where do they do they go first? Do they enter before or after the pupils? Do they make them wait or line up outside?

2. What are the teacher's first posture, gesture and statement; to whom are they addressed?

3. What effects are apparently intended? (Notice tone and loudness of voice, as well as what is said.)

4. How long is it before the lesson proper can begin? What things have happened up to this point?

5. Does the teacher seem to be a different kind of person inside classroom and out? How?

6. Assess the complexity of vocabulary and grammar used by the teacher. Do they match that used by the pupils in (1) their responses to the teacher, (2) their talk among themselves? The teacher's language may be precise, esoteric, everyday but accurate, or loose. Does the language used by the teacher elucidate the intended meanings or does it hinder them?

7. What does the teacher do when a child asks a question that reveals he has not understood the lesson? Does the teacher's language change at this point? How?

8. Are questions to pupils
   a) previously worked out
   b) spontaneous and exploratory
   c) implying an answer
   d) by several exchanges leading the pupils to the one answer expected?

9. Does the teacher use analogies? Do they communicate the point to the children?

10. Does the situation seem to be one of mutual communication between teacher and children? How do you assess this?

11. Does the teacher use many negated sentences as compared to positive sentences?

12. Is the teacher's voice being clearly perceived (i.e. do the pupils recognize the pronunciation as understandable even if the observer finds it difficult)?

13. Is the teacher pausing within and between sentences so as to make each clause, phrase etc. stand out? Does the voice modulation enhance the meanings, or disrupt them?

14. *Note*
Negated questions are about twice as difficult to comprehend as their positive equivalents.

Questions that demand descriptions (How? What? When?) are possible to reply to with about half the hesitation incurred by an interpretation question (Why?).

The number of hesitation pauses are proportional to the stress of the social situation.

15. How does the teacher register that the pupil's response is considered incorrect? What is the response of other pupils to the teacher's signal of incorrectness?

16. How does the teacher deal with the unexpected event?

17. In individual learning situations
    a) does the teacher get to all those needing help?
    b) does the teacher adjust his language and posture from child to child?

18. Does the teacher have particular postures and gestures which signal to the class that he is expecting a major change in activity?

19. How does the teacher use silences to communicate?

20. How does the teacher adjust this talk to different groups of children engaged in the same task?

D. RESOURCES

1. What books, tools, apparatus, equipment, materials etc. are available and where are they located and stored?

2. How are the tasks defined? (Worksheets, instructions, negotiation . . .)

3. To what extent do pupils and teachers have equal access to resources?

4. Is there any variation in the way that the task(s) are perceived by different groups of pupils?

5. If worksheets are being used
   a) do they specify a sequential programme of tasks, or
   b) do they attempt to initiate self-direction?

6. Are the questions asked of the teacher by the pupils related to
   a) difficulties in making sense of the worksheets
   b) the intended task
   c) extensions of the intended task?

Note

Some instructions that seem simple may be difficult in practice, e.g. requests for descriptions of smells, shapes, textures, orientation etc.

7. What is the school's buying policy for materials, equipment etc.?

8. What technical assistance is available?

9. What preparation was necessary for the particular lesson?

E. THE LESSON

1. What is its designation on the timetable?

2. Which department does it come under?

3. Who teaches it?

4. What is the aim of the lesson from the teacher's point of view?

5. How does it relate to a sequence or theme?

6. What is its logical structure in terms of content?

F. BACKGROUND INFORMATION ON THE SCHOOL

1. Name.

2. Type (direct grant, secondary modern, day/boarding . . .)

3. Sex composition.

4. Age range.

5. Size/intake.

6. Location (urban, suburban, rural . . .)

7. Denomination.

8. Staff size.

9. Number and size of departments.

10. School uniform.

11. Recent history (reorganization etc).

12. Parent-teacher organizations.

Documentation

See if there is a school history, if the school has old logbooks, back copies of school magazines. Look out for local newspaper clippings. Take advantage of opportunities to discuss the image of the school among parents, local residents etc.

Making a lesson profile

We suggest looking at one or two lessons in some detail in terms of their profiles. This is quite a time-consuming process, but by examining one or two lessons closely you will find that you develop a general insight that will help you in observing other lessons. Lessons can usually be described in terms of a brief sequence of events — they have a beginning, a middle and an end. For example:

1. Introduction — demonstration — practical — discussion — conclusion

2. Introduction — film — discussion — note-taking — summary

3. Introduction — presentation of work by groups — discussion — summary

etc. etc.

Often a single lesson only makes sense when it is seen as a sequence, so try and find out what has preceded it in the course, and what will follow. (You can try asking teacher *and* pupils about previous lessons and comparing their responses.) The teacher may be willing to tell you quite a lot about the lesson, about his general aims and objectives, and about the class in general. If you have the chance, compare topics of conversation and what he/she says before and after you have observed the lesson. After the lesson make a rough plan of what happened using the following illustrative scheme as a guide. With practice you will find you can record more easily and accurately, but don't let the process of recording get in the way of observing — only do it if you find it interesting.

NOTICE

1. What cues signal changes in activity and who initiates them.

2. How well formed, smooth and simultaneous these transitions are for different members of the class.

EXAMPLE 1

Science lesson, the first 15 minutes.

ROOM PLAN

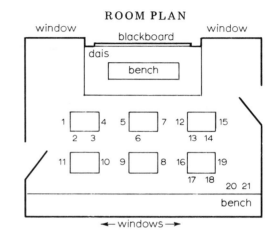

SPACES

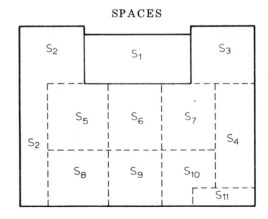

The profile of the first fifteen minutes of the science lesson (Example 1) appears quite straightforward and presents few problems. What is striking about it is how well ordered it all seems, how everyone seems to know what to do next. Given this kind of introduction to the lesson we would suggest it might be interesting to ask the pupils about the continuing course of the lesson — do they, for instance, start writing up the experiment before completing it? Do they know what kind of results they expect (or are expected) to get? Can they see the relationships between the experiment itself and the knowledge it is supposed to illuminate or create? What do they do when they get a 'wrong' result? When the teacher talks to them does he mainly ask questions? If so, how long is the average pupil response? What is the teacher's reaction to 'wrong' answers?

In other words, because a lesson seems unproblematic, even uneventful, it does not mean that there is nothing to observe. The essence of observation is the creation of insight out of what might seem initially to be routine and commonplace. Hidden beneath the surface of this lesson are unresolved issues which, when they are made visible, reveal possible alternative beliefs, values and practices.

LESSON PROFILE

Activity	0 minutes *Settling down*	5 minutes *Registration*	10 minutes *Introduction*	15 minutes *Practical*
Teacher	Chats to P5, 6, 9. Checks equipment with technician	Checks off pupils present	Lectures, asks questions of class. Recall of previous lesson and homework; intoduces practical task and gives rationale	Moves around room talking to groups
Pupils	Come in in groups, sit around chatting	Respond when called	Mostly attentive: 6, 7 talking, 13 writing, 18 gazing out of window	Working in twos and threes on experiment
Resources	None	None	Blackboard, white chalk	Test-tubes, reagents, glass tubing, bunsen burners
Noise level	Moderate	Quiet	Quiet	High
Use of space	T in S3 4, moving to S2, 1. P in S5, 6, 7. Sitting 8, 9, 10, 11	T in S1 Ditto	T in S1 Ditto	General, but no pupils in S1 or S3

EXAMPLE 2

The first two minutes of an English lesson (bottom stream, fourth year class, boys secondary modern school, north London).

OBSERVER'S NOTES
The class is in the state of subdued chaos typical of the beginnings and endings of lessons. Some boys are sitting on their desks, others are wrestling around, conversation is contained within several overlapping groups. The teacher comes in, puts his case on the desk at the front of the room and starts talking quietly to two of the boys who sit right in front of his desk. There is no marked change in behaviour as he comes into the room, but the more boisterous behaviour stops and boys start to gravitate towards their desks. Teacher then says, 'Right take out your books'. . . . During the next minute he gives one boy instructions to go to the reading teacher, and questions another boy about his books, he then says, 'Right then, page 72'. In the next fifteen seconds one boy asks him a question about his books (this conversation is not quite public as teacher indicates by the level and tone of his voice). Teacher then says, 'Right now if you are right,

you just put a tick in the margin, if you are wrong, you use a pencil to write in the correct word or words . . .'

COMMENT
'Getting the attention of the class' is problem for new teachers, and one we will return to again. Here we have a teacher in a difficult situation managing the problem almost invisibly.

PROFILE

Time (seconds)	0 15 30	45 60 75	90 105	120
Teacher	Enters room	'Take out your books'	'Right then, page 72'	Instructions
Boys	Different activities unco-ordinated	Move to desks; similar activities	Readiness	Quiet, attentive
Noise level	High	Moderate	Low	Very low

ROOM PLAN   (ground floor)

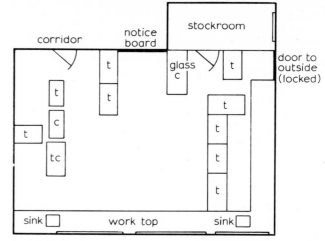

t   table
c   cupboard
tc 'tiger' cupboard (has a poster of an Esso tiger on it)

EXAMPLE 3
First year interdisciplinary inquiry at Fairlop Girls' School,
15 January 1970.

OBSERVER'S NOTES
*Two teachers, Miriam (art) and Ros (music), one student and
two classes in the art room for a whole afternoon. During the
week the children have been developing and preparing six
different dramatized incidents. During the afternoon these
are linked together using the idea of a 'time machine' to
relate disparate times and places. This leads to a decision to
pursue 'dreams' as a future theme.*

PROFILE

Time (minutes)	0	10	40	70	120	130 140
	Preface	Miriam introduces the idea of the time machine	Rehearsal and tuning up	Performance	Discussion and decision	Clearing up

20

OBSERVER'S NOTES (extracted to fill out profile)
Time (minutes)

9   *Miriam introduces the idea of a journey using OHP (overhead projector), Asks the time, fixes the co-ordinates of the room in time and space. Separates dimensions of time and space. Children become somewhat restless and impatient to 'start'.*

17 *Miriam: 'Everyone close your eyes a minute.' Hush descends. 'Start going through water right to the bottom of the sea. Hold it a minute. When you're at the bottom open your eyes and don't say anything at all.' Her voice drops. 'Sharon, mark on the time line how far from how your play was.'*
    Note: Miriam using a well-worn traditional teacher strategy to get attention but wholly integrated with the ideas of the lesson.

21 *'One person from each group tell us where your play happened,* when *it happened and* where *it happened.'*

32 *Miriam asks them to concentrate. 'Will you please stop talking Janice.'*

34 *Miriam has the plays plotted in time and space. 'We'll start with the ones here and now and work backwards.' Another group is set up to link the plays as a time traveller.*

36 *Groups break off to prepare their own plays.*

38 *Miriam works with one representative from each group sorting out the order of performance. Ros works with a group of musicians. Student working with a dance group. No children appear inactive or uninvolved. Noise high but not grating.*

55 *Rehearsal continues, the musicians tuning up. Moving furniture. Miriam and Ros much less in evidence talking briefly to groups of two and three rather than to large groups. Curtains are drawn and all but two lights are off. Everyone busy or waiting at their stations.*

70 *Ros formalizes by foghorning. Miriam shushes, noise drops rapidly. Ros asks for dead silence but this fails to penetrate some groups. Slowly it does. 'Everyone sitting down.' Chairs rearranged. All lights out. Performing the plays.*

72 *Janice's play is done by shadow play on a wall.*

75 *Second play. 'The sausage machine'.*

77½ *Link to next play. Noise low, no one has to shush. Another shadow play.*

80 *Play using OHP*

81 *Link.*

82 *Rhonda, Jill and Caroline. Play is long and rambling but audience intent.*

90 *Play is long, intricate and absorbing. A wild child who becomes socialized, a kind of* My Fair Lady.

91 *Audience still absolutely silent.*

103 *Play ends. Audience hum. Ros shushes into link.*

105 *Janice's play.*

112 *Ends.*

114 *Link.*

120 *End. Applause.*

Miriam retains formality, 'Stay sitting where you are'. Discussion of the idea. They feel it is still plays with links and not a coherent whole. Miriam suggests they need a device to give the feeling of time and space passing. They decide to develop this.

127 *A well, a tunnel, a dream, a wind, an adventure, a shipwreck, falling into a TV screen. Ros and Miriam*

*suggest a vote but Miriam changes her mind. Girls
protest so they revive the idea and vote.*

131 *Decision to pursue the idea of a dream. Miriam quietens
them down. Laying plans for next week.*

132 *Clearing up.*

TEACHER'S PROFILE (Miriam)

TABLE 1 — teacher's profile (Miriam)

	Before	*Start*	*Rehearsal*	*Play*	*Discussion*	*Clearing up*
My activity	Informal chat. Some direction of activity re collection of equipment	Semi-didactic discussion/ lecture to ascertain the comprehension of particular part	Helping with ideas and problems with equipment. Conveying information. Encouraging activity among those reluctant	Watching. Helping with odd equipment and queries. Altering what happened by passing written messages to particular people	Adding to ideas already brought up by Ros. Encouraging new ideas from kids. Helping to take vote on idea for next week	Seeing that equipment put back, that room left tidy. Listening with half an ear to other ideas
Children's activity	Seating themselves. Talking. Making inquiries as to the nature of the afternoon's activity. Moving about. Slow flow of children into classroom	Some listening. Some restlessly whispering. Some quietly carrying on with written work	Heavily involved in preparing their ideas physically and mentally	Watching with a high degree of intensity. Acting out their ideas. Janice and Susan acting as a link. Using me and Ros to confirm ideas. Acting on messages	Quiet, controlled but very lively interest and contribution	Some taking equipment back, some helping to clear up. A milling around and breakdown of activity
Concentration level	Low	Low	High	Very high	High	Low

TABLE 1 — (cont.)

	Before	Start	Rehearsal	Play	Discussion	Clearing up
Noise level	Fairly high	Low but mumbly	Very high	Extremely quiet except for actors. Quiet talk at breaks	Moderate	Fairly high
No. of children involved	—	20 really involved. 6—7 uninvolved. Rest restless and half involved	All except 3—4 opters-out	All — either as audience or actors	All	—
Space used	General. Many sitting on table tops but some using tables for work	Mostly centre. Some use of tables for continued work	Everywhere! Including stock cupboard	Centre of room as 'stage', moving in breaks	Rather more compact	General wandering
Equipment used	None	Chart, pencil, postcard	Furniture, dressing-up clothes, paper, scissors, pins, sellotape, string, paint, felt-tips, gels, OHP, screen, Aldis (slide projector), percussion instruments	None	None	
Movement — children	Fluctuating to talk to friends. Arrivals seeking places, exits for equipment	Fairly static, children seated	Moving *to* an area to practise. Moving *out* for advice, materials	Restricted to actors. Changing over. Moving to see screen	Very little not so much movement to Ros and me	Fluctuating
Movement — me	Concentrated near tiger cupboard	In front of tiger cupboard facing group	From group to group. Quite a long time in the stock cupboard	Less. Specific movements to give messages. Long spells of watching	In front of class but as part of group	About room

NOTES

Before the start: I was aware at the time that this crucial thing was badly handled partly because IMMJ (class number) came in in dribs and drabs because of litter rota duty, but also because I hadn't thought of a better way of using the time, i.e. dressing up for the work. The children just lolled about chatting, waiting for us to start.* This may have added to the restlessness because they were not expecting us to expect them to listen in this way. There was no previous conditioning. The making of a chart was in keeping with the form but is probably too academic a way of establishing a concept — besides which it was a very feeble chart. If I had prepared a basic one beforehand it would have been much easier. The concentration exercise worked quite well — perhaps if this was the best way of putting over the point an exercise of this nature should have been done first. Having tried this method I doubt its validity in so large a group, when 'groupness' is of value in itself. It has an alienating influence in terms of creative ideas.

The content was chosen to meet the need for a device to bring all the work of the previous week together. We had felt that some kind of forming or formalization could be useful, maybe towards the concentration of an idea that wasn't narrow. As the ideas (of the plays) had seemed so various I thought that a link made by a journey through time and space might suffice. We also thought that some consideration of the relationships of these elements towards the formation of a general concept, apart from the afternoon's work, would not go amiss at this time.

*This has parallels with other IDE (Interdisciplinary enquiry) time, though for different reasons. The aimlessness at the beginning of Monday IDE, for instance, is caused by the problems for the girls of starting themselves off or having an idea at all.

Almost from the start I felt that the idea and method of putting the work together wasn't the best way. But once I had embarked upon it I had to go on.

I think that the idea of things in some kind of chronological sequence did get across. The method of connecting them was rather turgid though. In retrospect I think that offering it to them as a problem to work out, say, 'How could the themes be linked?' would have worked better — then maybe a vote on the best after a report-back session.

The aspect of the simultaneousness of time/space relationships did not come across at all. Perhaps it would have been better to have seen it as a device and no more. Perhaps this was not the time to exploit them — though I can now see ways I might.

That they were expected to do something different, to behave in unexpected ways with us, is I believe of value in itself as a stimulus. As Ros said they might have been quiet for someone they were used to, but this wouldn't mean they would have listened. In a way perhaps I should have demanded it till I got it — but it would perhaps have ruined the rest of the day.

IN RETROSPECT

The events of this afternoon seemed at the time to be somewhat lacking in fluency. Miriam's notes indicate that she was not entirely happy with the early part of the lesson. In retrospect it appeared a critical lesson — it was the point at which the children seemed to realize that they could take some responsibility for activities. The idea of 'doing plays' had been theirs and they had been able to pursue it, but the sequence of events on 'dreams' that followed this afternoon turned out to be highly active, creative and rewarding for teachers and children.

Different perspectives

In presenting these three examples of the use of profiles, a problem has arisen. How different are teacher's and observer's accounts of the same lesson? This becomes especially clear in the third example, for although teacher's and observer's accounts do not actually conflict they do reveal differences in concern. The observer's task is to present as precisely as he can an account of events as they happen — the teacher's concern is with the quality of performance, with alternative ways of managing events. What seems to an observer to be a relatively stable, concrete, socially structured series of events seems to the teacher to be fluid, fluctuating, transient and fragile. In many ways what is straightforward to one is problematic for the other.

We want to emphasize the importance of trying to incorporate into the idea of observation the attempt to get inside the perspective of the participants. Too often the word is used loosely to mark out a passive role — you 'sit back and observe', simply letting sensations wash over you. No doubt there is some value in this, but we also want to emphasize the importance of complementing 'objective' descriptions and 'subjective' impressions with the continuous attempt to see events as they are seen by those participating in them. Don't only *watch* the teacher; try and get inside his head. Try, temporarily, to suspend your judgement and instead to empathize with both teacher and children.

Plans and profiles

The aim of doing the profile is to try and give you a way of developing some feeling for the 'structure' of lessons. Most teachers are aware of the fact that they try to organize lessons so that different segments of the lesson create different kinds of 'atmosphere', and in such a way that these different segments articulate as a meaningful whole. Like a piece of music, a good lesson can have different 'movements' which have various, contrasting moods but which taken as a sequence form a cumulative experience.

Teachers often talk about teaching as being similar to acting, but our feeling is that what they mean by this is that they find themselves projecting themselves differently according to the situation. The teacher cannot escape himself (or herself) in the same way that some actors can. In fact what many beginning teachers find most difficult about teaching is that they seem to be vulnerable and exposed in much the same way as an entertainer or performer, but with few of the protective devices that such professionals can use to insulate 'onstage' from 'offstage'.

Used effectively, the profile should give you a means of slightly distancing yourself from the action, so that instead of seeing this as undifferentiated experience you can begin to see it as a sequence of events. One of the most difficult things for beginning teachers to appreciate seems to be a sense of timing — for them lessons often appear to be frozen in time, perpetual instants. One result is that they talk too long, too much or not enough, that they misjudge the time required to initiate or establish an activity, or to clear away, or they let some practical task go on too long for what they want to develop out of it.

The problem is not solved by reference to the clock — for the 'time' we are talking about refers to the number and pacing and intensity of different events. It is a question of judging, in particular contexts, how long to talk to a whole class in such a way as to concentrate and focus their interest and motivation, but to avoid losing it or causing it to be directed to non-task activities. It is about creating a climate in which interest can be quickened or slowed according to the needs of the moment. Notice, for example, in the third profile, how Miriam manages to slow down the tempo and concentrate the interest of the class by using the imaginative exercise of making them close their eyes and 'travel through water'.

Most tutors encourage their students to plan out lessons in advance and to record how they went in practice. In this way it is possible to get some feeling of the mismatch between plans and actions. What we want to encourage is an extension of this planning so that you become better able to respond yourself to the situations that you create as a result of your plans. Just because your lesson plan says you hope to talk to the whole class for ten minutes before releasing them to some practical task does not mean that you need to stick to that as a commitment. You are not necessarily a better teacher simply for being able to predict your actions. The difficulty is in responding with some sensitivity to the situations you have engineered, because it is too easy, having *established* the situations, to feel responsible and protective towards them. If the class arrives excited from PE, or excited from having spent a double period in the company of a highly repressive teacher, you will have to respond to that mood rather than stick to the letter of your plans. The essence of teaching is the creation and management of situations for communication and learning.

The aim of the profile is to give you a means of studying the kinds of situations that are created in school classrooms. Just how these can be used we suggest in the second part of this book.

The observer observed

One of the difficulties of teaching practice is being observed. In a sense, as any new teacher is, students are scrutinized by the children, but they also have to learn to tolerate observation by other teachers, perhaps the head or head of department, college tutors and even external examiners. In many colleges this difficulty is further compounded by the fact that many of these observers are present with evaluative functions — trying to fit you into a category of comparative merit. (A process incidentally that is indefensible bureaucratically and educationally and runs counter to sixty years of the findings of research.) In this book we have assumed that the use of observation — as a means of making judgements of merit — is hardly defensible; when that merit is essentially comparative we think it is impossible to defend.

So much for our own values. We have never been in a position where we had to judge teachers in terms of merit. Those who do, however much they criticize the practice, often have difficulty in preventing themselves from coming to believe that their judgements are justifiable. The situation remains that many students are judged, and many tutors judge them, without either of them feeling entirely happy about the system or its procedures, and this exerts considerable constraints and prevents much collaboration between students and tutors. Our aim here is not to attack the system but to try and say something helpful to those who have to live with it.

Get whoever observes your lessons to talk about what they see. Don't be content with trivial, unhelpful comments like, 'You seem to be doing all right'. Get them to talk about what they saw. Use your own experience of observation and the observation points in this book as a means of formulating specific questions. If necessary adopt the stance of interviewer, asking all the time for instances and examples. Don't let the observer ramble off into anecdotes or unnecessary theory, but keep him/her to the point. If this proves difficult ask for comments about particular children or particular incidents.

This does not mean you need to adapt a belligerent attitude; if you avoid *telling* him and concentrate on getting *his* perspective you are more likely to impress him than to antagonize him.

On the whole it is best to avoid apologizing or explaining what you feel were your mistakes, or arguing with the observer's interpretations when you disagree with them. The best way of handling disagreements is by presenting counter-examples, more or less without comment. In this way you can remain outside the argument. Once you start using personal statements and interpretations the argument itself becomes personal. Keep your personal identity at some distance from the discussion — treat it as a professional consultation.

Don't be afraid to negotiate about which lessons should be observed. If you feel things are going badly in a class tell your tutor, or the teacher, that you would like them to observe in order to help, or conversely that you would prefer it if they didn't. If you feel yourself in difficulties, ask for help, but try to ask in a way that invites response. In other words, before the lesson discuss with the observer what might be most interesting to observe. If the observer takes notes of any kind ask if you can have a copy for your own use.

A note for tutors

For any observer it is something of a privilege to be allowed to observe a lesson, and the least you can do in return is to share your perceptions and interpretations with the teacher. Just because student teachers have observers imposed upon them does not mean that this obligation is lessened.

This book is *not* about education

Those of us who work in teacher education are caught in a dilemma; the demands of the job take us in two different directions simultaneously.

On the one hand we owe it to our students to help fit them into the present school system with the minimum stress on them and the schools. They have a lot at stake and most, more than anything else, need to feel confident that at the end of their course they will be able to hold down a job as a teacher with some ease.

On the other hand most of us also have ideas about 'education' which only partially relate to our experience of schools. We need to be careful that we do not fall into two traps. One comes from thinking that our own ideals represent the *real* essence of education — so stunting our imagination in novel situations because of our inability to understand alternative values. Another comes from expecting our students to realize in practice the very values we have failed to act upon ourselves.

It is very easy for education lecturers both to promote one educational ideal as religion, and to promote sets of values and practices as feasible that they have not lived through themselves.

We are caught then between training students to enter the existing system (in all its variety and complexity) as competent teachers, and wanting to promote particular ideas and values within (or even outside) that system. There can be few of us who have not, in that tension, met conflicts and decisions that were only resolved with difficulty.

This book is not about education because it only looks at a part of what it means to be a teacher. Essentially it is a book for student teachers showing how they might research schools and classrooms in ways that make it easier for them to ease themselves into a teaching role — it is about *teaching*, not about *how to teach*.

27

We felt the book was necessary because it seemed to us that 'teaching' was a neglected subject in many education courses. What we hope it will do is to give teachers ways of understanding the realities of their own schools and classrooms. Only when teachers are able to do that are alternative ideas of education possible. You have to have some means of describing your own situation before you can attempt to change it. The quality and effectiveness of your attempts at change are directly related to the quality of your understanding.

There are people, including many teachers and students, who would like to see education courses much more strongly biased towards teaching. Obviously we hope that the ideas we have presented could be used in such courses. We should add, however, that in all our attempts to put them into practice we have discovered that it has often been the informal aspects of activities that have been most valuable; the chance for students and children to meet on neutral ground. In our experience it is when students and children work together in situations (out of school) where neither has responsibility for the other that mutual understandings are reached.

One student at Chelsea, Ann Fiander, was impressed by the book *Young Teachers and Reluctant Learners* by Hannam Smyth and Stephenson (Penguin, 1971) and attempted a similar project with a group of children in the school she was sent to on teaching practice. Her account raises all the problems of trying to articulate personal identity with the kind of social identity required by the school, and this becomes very clear when she describes her relationships with a group of children who lived on her street:

During the Easter holidays I found a West Indian boy writing down the numbers of the houses. When I inquired what he was doing he informed me he was bored so he was adding up the numbers. I asked what they usually did. Well they had run round the alleys all morning and perhaps mum would take them to the park later. Then he said 'You're a teacher, you taught my brother in the primary school. Can you give us something to do?' By this time there were four of assorted sizes under ten years of age. So I asked them into the garden and we did some origami.

After that the group grew to ten. The ages ranging from eleven to three (he came with his sister who was six). They asked if I had books and could they look at them. The eldest girls, Sheena (eleven), Katie (ten) and Carol (eight) took Thirty-six Children *and Tolkien's* Lord of the Rings *away to read as that was the nearest to children's books I had. They came along quite regularly during the holiday. Our work included hunting for wild flowers and plants around the area; we made a press and Sheena made a book into which she stuck the flowers and wrote a little about each one. The younger members of the group made drawings of the flowers and either wrote stories about them if they could write or copied what they had asked me to write for them. During the Easter holidays they came round nearly every day to play with my hi-fi system, the tape recorder, to write or draw, or do origami.*

I did not expect to see them again once school had started but they came in the evenings. One evening I was just about to start my dinner when three of them arrived. I apologized saying 'I am sorry, I am just about to have my dinner.' 'Oh, don't worry, we don't mind, we've had our tea,' was their reply. I was dealing with the simple minds of children not the socialized double talk of adults, so I let them in. I was amazed to find they knew what they had come to do and quitely settled down to do it.

My suggestion that we went fishing for minibeasts in a stream one Sunday met with approval and we made fishing nets on the Saturday. It poured with rain on Sunday and I did not expect them to turn up, but four children arrived on the doorstep at the specified time and could not understand why I should contemplate not going. We went. We got soaked but they did not notice and had to be persuaded to go home after about one and a half hours. At first they complained that there were no fish but once they discovered the mud was full of creatures they were overjoyed. We went home and dried out and then examined the mud. Katie drew many of the animals and described them.

I was amazed at the interest these children took. Later in May I said I no longer had the time in the evenings to work with them because of this dissertation. Sheena and Katie came round to say if I let them come in they would not disturb me. They brought work and often stayed till 8.00 or 9.00 in the evening. They asked me if I could help them with some of their work and often asked for ideas but worked quietly for most of the time. Sheena started a project on Shakespeare but the only book I had was one of quotations. I do not believe she read through it but she certainly learnt some of the more popular pieces of his plays like the witches' song from Macbeth. 'I've picked out the best bits', she informed me when I asked how she was managing.

Katie, a 10 year old West Indian, began to show a real ability to draw. After we had been out to look at the house martins one evening she came in and began to draw them from my bird book. She requested criticism asking what was wrong with the bird she had drawn. I suggested that its wing was not quite correct and she altered it. My own artistic talents are nil but when a friend suggested I tried to get her to draw bottles or fruit as still lifes, I tried it out. I explained and showed her the highlights and shadows on a milk bottle and told her to shade them in. After three abortive attempts (my inability to explain rather than her artistic ability) she began to understand what I meant and went on to draw a reasonable still life. I only hope they spot and exploit this talent at school, not let it go to waste like Lizeth's musical ability.

The rest of the group, who had been banned while I worked because they were noisy, returned saying they would be good. What was even more surprising was that they were. I never thought 6 and 8 year olds could be so quiet and creative. They often worked for over an hour before beginning to get restless. They made collages or drew or got the elder children or me to write sentences for them. When they got restless they would ask 'Can we go now please?'. 'Yes of course', I would reply, 'Can we come back though?' they would always ask on the way out.

Ann Fiander, 'What does education achieve: a case study of a teacher and six pupils'. GCSE dissertation, Chelsea College, 1973.

An ideal education course (for us) would be one based on two kinds of research. Students would research schools and classrooms, perhaps in the ways we have suggested; but they would also research children — mainly out of classes and out of school. We have not described this second kind of research because we only have slight experience of organizing it. But we feel confident enough in what we have done to suggest that given an education course based on these two kinds of research most of what usually passes as educational studies or educational theory could be happily left until well after pre-service training.

This book though is not primarily about what we think *should* happen in schools, but about what we think *does* happen.

Studying the school

Most of this book has been about classrooms, but in order to understand what goes on in classrooms you will find it necessary sooner or later to look at the school as a whole.

Once you have some idea of how to construct a lesson profile you will find that this raises the problem of how the profile came to take the form it did. This will mean asking questions about the allocation and distribution of resources, about timetabling, about organization, about the intake, and about the ideas, values and attitudes of staff.

What we recommend is that you approach these problems from an understanding, based on observation, of the school at work. This is why we started with classroom observation and with the lesson profile rather than with the school as a whole.

One of the first people you are likely to meet in school is the headmaster or headmistress. In a small primary school you are likely to meet the head every day and by the end of your teaching practice to feel you know him/her well. In a large urban comprehensive you may only see the head once in a term, and come to perceive him or her as a distant figure.

Inevitably during the course of the term you will learn how the head is seen by other members of staff and by the children. You will hear about particular disputes and decisions, and perhaps about his/her earlier career. The head may be willing to talk to you, and it is certainly worth asking if you can talk about what the job involves and how decisions are taken. Heads have very different styles, but try to find out from the head how decisions are made about school structure. (Are classes mixed ability or is there some form of streaming? Is there a house system? What are the main departments of the school?) Ask about finance — how much money does the school have each year? What needs to be paid for? How is it divided? Ask about policy — how does he/she see the future of the school? How does the school relate to other local schools? To the community? Ask about administration and control — how does the head see the LEA? How often does he see the Chief Education Officer? What does he see as the role of advisers, teacher's centres, local colleges of education? Ask about curriculum — is the school involved in any curriculum development projects? How did this involvement come about? What have been the main issues and problems?

In primary schools you can ask more detailed questions — about how particular reading schemes were selected, for example. In secondary schools you will have to ask heads of departments for this kind of information.

If you have the time and energy, talk to everyone you can about the school. Most schools will be helpful if you are a student on teaching practice. Don't be frightened to ask. Most people are happy to talk about what their work involves and many schools now have teachers doing quite unusual jobs — school counsellors, directors of studies, advisory teachers and so on. Don't set out to antagonize people but try to listen. Try and cross-check what different people tell you about the same issues. Above all listen to what everyone has to say — technicians, caretakers, secretaries all have their views of the school which are likely to be different from those of both teachers and pupils.

On confidentiality

As a student it is perhaps best not to attempt to tape-record interviews or conversations. But it is still necessary to keep some information to yourself. Don't gossip, and don't pass on what might seem confidential information. You will soon establish yourself as someone trustworthy if you are careful about what you say.

This applies to information about children and parents as much as about staff. Students have created embarrassing situations by talking about children or teachers on the bus home, not knowing who was listening in the seat behind.

One student observed that teachers who talked about children in the staffroom seemed to him to be breaking confidence. Teachers who had close relationships with children, in that school, didn't talk about them to other teachers in public — the staffroom.

A note on questionnaires

Questionnaires are much more difficult to design, administer and process than most people realize. If you try to use them on school practice you are likely to end up learning a lot about questionnaires and very little about the school.

If you do decide to use a questionnaire you will need professional help — not least about the protocol required in getting permission from heads, LEAs, parents and children.

Perhaps the best form of questionnaire is one designed and administered by pupils as part of the curriculum of the school. But still be warned! There are many dangers in the use of questionnaires in schools, and issues of research methodology are the most minor. One of the most useful surveys is the sociometric survey — but again take advice and take care. It is quite a good idea to collect school documents . . .

New toilet arrangements

1. Open only at break and lunchtime.
2. At break all toilets except East Quadrangle toilet (Management Block) will be open.
3. At lunchtime only toilets on Pb level will be open.

If a boy needs a toilet in an emergency he must contact the Nurse with a note from his teacher.

Headmaster

(From a London school, December 1973.)

Form Teas

    ... Give a list of the things you need to the pantry the night before. Ask the under matron for table cloths and keep them for both teas. If you make toast, see that the kitchen is properly cleaned up. Don't make toast yourself. You must seat the most senior person on your right (if you sit round a table). After give a little food to the Lower VI. Don't let the others take food to their bedrooms etc.

Sunday Teas

    If you have toast it is better not to allow Lower VIth in with you. Miss Ellison made this a pre's privilege.

(From a Head Girl's book.)

EARRINGS
BAN ON
BOYS UPHELD

THE REV GEORGE PARR, chairman of the governors of Ripon Secondary Modern School, West Riding, last night 'heartily endorsed' the action of the headmaster, Mr Joseph Cooper, in refusing to allow boys wearing earrings into classrooms.

Two pupils, Stephen Anderson of Knaresborough Road, Ripon, and Michael Tiffany, of Victoria Avenue, Ripon, both aged 16, have been barred from lessons for refusing to remove gold earrings.

Anderson has been absent from school for more than a fortnight, but two other boys who joined his protest returned to school yesterday without earrings.

Mr Cooper, who was appointed headmaster in September with a mandate to tighten discipline among the 820 pupils, said: 'I like to see earrings on women but on boys they are effeminate. Because their ears are pierced they could be a hazard when tempers flare or on the sports field.'

Mr Parr said: 'I emphasized at the interviews for the headmaster's post that there was a need to strengthen discipline at the school.' He added that legal action might be taken if the boys continued their action.

PUPILS SENT HOME
Hair too long

Many boys were turned away from St Kevin's Roman Catholic Secondary School, Leeds, yesterday because their hair was considered too long by the headmaster, Mr Alfred Mitchell. For some, it was the third consecutive morning that they had been barred.

(Daily Telegraph, December 1973)

Interviewing pupils

In some schools it will be expected that you should talk fairly informally to individuals and small groups of children. In other schools it will be expected that all relationships between teachers and pupils should be formalized.

For those who do have the opportunity to talk informally to children, in or out of classes, we have included in the 'Observation resource book' some notes on how to interview children.

Documentation

In some courses students are asked to produce case studies of both the school and of individual children. They may even be assessed on this work. As a style of research, case study demands that you present selected observations in such a way as to describe an individual or an institution, trying to keep your own ideas and feelings as controlled as possible. Few good professional case studies exist in education to refer to as models, though we recommend Barry MacDonald's studies of the Humanities Curriculum Project, Roger Graef's film for BBC TV and Louis Smith's study in one classroom. Those interested in pursuing this style of research will find further information in the 'Observation resource book'.

We do, however, recommend that you attempt to document your observations even if this is not formally required by the course. Even when it is a requirement of the course it may be useful to keep a second set of notes for your eyes only (see, for example, Nicholas Otty's book, *Learner Teacher*). We would not want documentation to become a routine chore, but our own experience has been that careful documentation almost always leads to insights which have the effect of leading you to see new facets to routine situations. Whenever documentation or recording becomes uninteresting and seems to be an end in itself, unrelated to real situations, stop unless it is a requirement of the course.

By documenting we don't simply mean writing things down. We would include the collection of any material that might seem trivial within the context of the school, but which outside or back at college might create valuable evidence for discussion. One student we know brought into a discussion group thirty self-portraits by the members of his class. Children's drawings, paintings and writings, lists of school rules, notes from parents, speeches given at speech day, lists of equipment, work sheets prepared by teachers, can all provide you with useful data.

One technique we have found productive, and which helps bypass note-taking, is for students on their return to college to interview each other on tape about their impressions and experiences. If the interviews are done in threes and are public to the group then they become cumulative and can provide a useful way not only of recording, but of presenting and sharing information.

On failure

The essential problem for most students going out on teaching practice is that they already know too much to be able to observe. Observation demands a certain naïveté, an ability to create the unexpected and unusual out of the commonplace and mundane. For many students the life of classrooms is only too familiar, and it is not the *events* of the classroom that are problematic but their own identity in relation to those events. The successes and crises are not seen as mere incidents but as personal achievements. The experience is often an experience of self.

By the age of twenty, someone who has been in full-time education since the age of five will have spent some 15,000 hours in educational establishments of one kind or another, and much of that time will have been spent in classrooms situations. It is difficult to think of any other arena in which we invest so much of our lives, so much so that it is difficult for us to estimate just what effect the experience has had in making us the people we are. Our ideas of success and failure, competition and co-operation, loyalty and independence — the values and beliefs that often seem to lie beyond our awareness and control — owe much to our years in school.

We mention this here for two reasons. One is that it is very easy in discussing teaching with beginning teachers to talk as though teaching is merely a question of learning a set of techniques.

Attempts to implement these 'techniques' that do not lead to the desired effects can create in beginning teachers a sense of failure of identity. The feeling is that if you are doing everything right but still the situation is wrong, then it must be your weakness as a person which underlies the problem.

The second reason is that teaching practice is for many students a time of trial. Nearly all of their educational experience will have been based on a notion of themselves as passive recipients of knowledge. They will have learnt to be reflective, to act minimally in educational settings in order to create an adequate impression, to carve off large pieces of their identity which surface only in other, out-of-school settings. Students in the classroom setting are typically restrained, even non-involved, wary and distanced from the action. But as teachers they are suddenly immersed in situations where they can no longer maintain that kind of detached, analytic stance. Whole areas of their identity which were previously kept out of classroom life are suddenly brought into it. Feelings, often quite intense feelings of love, fear, jealousy and hatred, which they have not felt since infant school, can suddenly be mobilized against children or other teachers.

Note the posters painted on walls. Collect documents, timetables, examples of children's work.

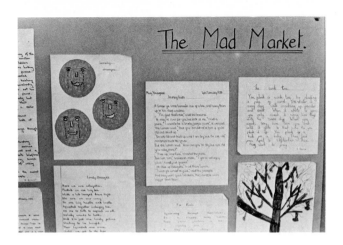

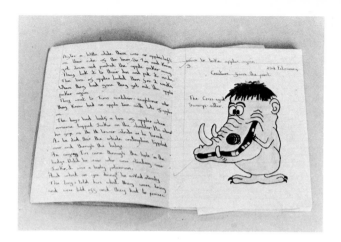

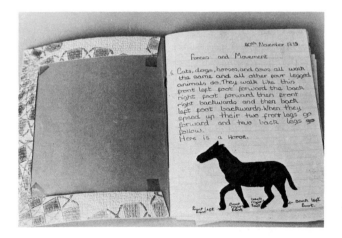

Many students manage the passage of identity from learner to teacher without personal difficulty. But we would guess that for most it is something of a personal crisis, one in which childhood and adolescent feelings about school need to be replayed and resolved if the student is going to synthesize a new identity. Some never reach that point; for many it happens during the first year of teaching after training; for some it happens in the first morning of the first teaching practice.

There is currently much debate in teacher education about making courses relevant and practical. We take this to mean that teachers want to face these kinds of issues — they want to face the problems of identity we have raised here. Particular concerns with control, communication and learning are secondary to the central issue of how you become yourself in the classroom.

In teacher education, as in many other areas of education, what is transmitted most effectively to the learner is a sense of personal worth; any sort of educational failure can be a crushing and humiliating experience. In teaching we all fail; there are always some children we fail to reach, some situations we mismanage, some mistakes we make. The more risks we take, the more mistakes we make, but the more we learn.

To say that this book is about self-discovery would be over-romantic — there is already enough romanticism in education to more than obscure the truth. Our idea about observation is not simply that students should watch good practice to see how to do it. Teaching isn't like that — it is an expression of the person, and anything as contrived as aping a successful teacher is a recipe for failure. Teaching isn't mechanistic, a matter of simply turning in an adequate performance. It is human communication, and concerns the way in which you perceive, and are perceived, act and react in the social situations created within educational organiza-tions. It's been said that as a sport, swimming exercises all the muscles in the body. Teaching is a kind of social equivalent of swimming — if you do it seriously it activates every fibre of perception and action in the person.

The Observation Resource Book

Almost as important as observation per se is the requirement of keeping an open mind about what we see. Our ways of looking at classrooms should not be unnecessarily restricted by prior assumptions about what should be going on there, nor even . . . by the seemingly logical link between the abstract processes of teaching and learning. In short, we must be prepared and willing to give up many of our comfortable beliefs about what classroom life is all about.

Philip Jackson
(*Life in Classrooms*)

Section 1. Analysing the profiles

The idea of producing lesson profiles is to try and find a way of ordering all the different events that go on during a lesson. It is a way of producing a coded reconstruction of classroom activities so that we can begin to talk about what goes on with some common reference to perception and understanding. Having got into the habit of thinking of lessons as a structured sequence of events it is not always necessary to produce the profile — it is intended as a means of understanding events rather than as an end product in itself.

Having established this approach we want to introduce some ideas that we found useful in observing lessons. We want to work towards a descriptive language which we can use to explore how lessons are at the same time both similar and different. The collection of ideas we are going to introduce is not an absolute one — the ideas are open to discussion, extension, addition and change — but we think it makes a useful starting point.

1. FORMAL AND INFORMAL SITUATIONS

If you look through a few lesson profiles you will notice that some of the changes in activity are marked quite dramatically. Usually these involve the teacher attracting the attention of the class in some way, perhaps at the start of the lesson or after an episode of practical work. Different teachers have different methods for managing these overall changes in group activity — consider this rather unusual method from a teacher's account of her infants' class:

There is, however, in the following pages, something left out: I didn't talk about discipline. An overall reflection of that work in the prefab could well give teachers a valid suspicion of chaos with the freedom of movement and talk. But chaos has a certain quality of its own that none of us allows in teaching; chaos presupposes a lack of control, whereas control was my first intention. As my inspector at tha. time observed, 'Discipline is a matter of being able to get attention when you want it.'

I often wanted attention and I wanted it smartly. And I trained the children in a way that is new only, maybe, in degree. Most teachers have some simple way of calling a room to attention; some use a bell, some rap a ruler, and most, I should think, use their voices. But where the sounds of learning and living are allowed in a room, a voice would need to be lifted and sharpened and could be unrepresentative of a gentle teacher; so, predictably, I used the keyboard. No crashing chord, no alarming octave, but eight notes from a famous master; the first eight notes from Beethoven's Fifth Symphony. What was good for him was good enough for me, since, whereas he demanded attention for the rest of the symphony from several thousand people, I wanted it for only a sentence.

At the sound of these notes I trained the Little Ones, whatever they were doing, to stop and look at me. I trained them this way from necessity but in time I did so from pleasure. And never through those vital years in the heaving prefab did I cease to be impressed at the sudden draining away of sound, like blood from a face, into the utmost silence. And not just silence, but stillness; every eye on me, every hand poised; an intensity of silence born from sound . . .

For me to speak and be heard by all.

Some simple direction, some needed advice indisputably heard by all.

How I polished this instrument of attention! My most valuable too, the most indispensable of them.

For it is not so much the content of what one says as the way in which one says it. However important the thing you say, what's the good of it if not heard or, being heard, not felt? To feel as well as hear what someone says requires whole attention. And that's what the master's command gave me — it gave me whole attention. You might argue, 'But how could a child at the far end of a room full of movement, talk and dance hear eight soft single notes?' Any teacher could answer that. The ones near the piano did. And they'd touch the others and tell the others until the spreading silence itself would tell, so that by the time the vibration of the strings had come to rest, so had the children. Those silences and those stillnesses, I'll remember them . . . for more than seven years after.

Sylvia Ashton-Warner, *Teacher* (Penguin, 1966).

This account implies two quite different kinds of teaching situation for the teacher in this class. One where there is 'freedom of movement and talk' and the teacher is relatively unobtrusive; the other where there 'is not just silence, but stillness; every eye on me, every hand poised'. It is the distinction between these two quite different kinds of classroom situation we consider most basic in understanding the profiles and which we want to explore in some detail.

A useful point to start looking at this difference is to look at the transitions between the situations, rather than at the situations themselves. To look at what Sylvia Ashton-Warner calls 'getting attention'.

Towards the end of a science practical lesson. The teacher walks to the front of the room and stands in front of the demonstration bench. He waits for the class to notice he is waiting for them to notice him. Gradually the ripple of attention spreads.

0 seconds   6 seconds   14 seconds   18 seconds   22 seconds

Can you sit down in your seats please   (Pause 4—10 seconds)   We're waiting for some people at the back

26 seconds   30 seconds   32 seconds   36 seconds   40 seconds

(Pause 14—34 seconds)   Oh look you two boys — do you really want me to start getting angry about it?   (Pause 40—2 seconds)

40

44 seconds *48 seconds* *52 seconds* *56 seconds* *60 seconds*

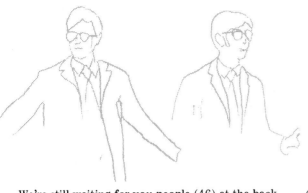

We're still waiting for you people (46) at the back

(Pause 50—6 seconds)

Right, now. Now that you're (60) all
sitting down could you all look
this way (62) please.

64 seconds *68 seconds* *72 seconds* *76 seconds*

(Pause 64—74 seconds)

Thank you. Now then.
Someone asked me a very
good question. They said
why can't we just carry on
mucking around with all
these things. Why do we
have to write it all down.

For a similar example see the film *School* mentioned at the back of the 'Resource book' — at the start of Mrs Dobson's first lesson with the class.

41

Although established teachers usually have some salient action for 'attracting the attention of the class', beginning teachers soon learn that the effectiveness of these actions is not dependent on any simple learning theory. The children do not respond to the signal like Pavlov's dogs in a simple 'stimulus-response' manner, but see the signal only in the context of that teacher's total performance. Another teacher simply mimicking the action cannot guarantee the same response.

Consider this extract from Jacob Kounin's research study:

Concern with discipline techniques may be as prevalent as it is because misbehaviour does stand out perceptually. While observing a classroom, one is more likely to notice a child who is throwing crayons than a child who is going about the business of writing in his workbook. And a teacher who is reprimanding a pupil is more likely to be noticed than when she is listening to a child read. Furthermore, there is no questioning the fact that one may observe a desist technique that is effective as well as observe a desist technique that is ineffective, especially if these occur in different classrooms. Thus, we have seen Teacher A walk to the light switch and flick the lights on and off two times as a signal for the children to be quiet and listen to her. It worked. The children immediately stopped talking or doing whatever they were doing, and sat in a posture of attention facing the teacher. Is this because of the teacher's light switching technique, or because there were other, and perhaps less immediately discernible, managerial techniques that produced a prevailing climate in this classroom that resulted in this technique, or any other, being effective? The following day, we observed Teacher B in the same school and same grade also walk to the light switch and flick the lights on and off as a signal for quiet and attention. It didn't work. The children who were talking continued to talk, two boys

who were poking each other continued their horseplay, and so on. These are merely single examples. The Videotape research and the High School Interviews and Questionnaires do not deny that some desists are effective and that others are ineffective. These studies do justify the statement that whether a desist is effective or ineffective is not dependent upon the qualities of the desist technique as such (except for anger producing discomfort) but rather upon other dimensions of classroom management, related commitments, or prevailing variables.

J. S. Kounin, *Discipline and Group Management in Classrooms* (Holt, 1970), pp. 72—3.

One teacher mimicking the actions of another has different effects — because for the children the action is not perceived as a discrete unit but is seen only in the context of accumulated knowledge about the teachers, the class and the school. The important thing at this point is not to reject the idea of analysis and reduce everything to 'personality of the teacher' arguments. What we need is a kind of analysis that relates actions to their contexts rather than leaving them isolated from the very things that give them meaning.

At this point it is clear that we have raised a number of crucial theoretical problems. What we are suggesting is that the classroom is a kind of action setting which in some ways is unlike most of the other settings with which we are familiar,* and that in some respects it has its own rules and its own logic. Both commonsense knowledge and formal psychology derived from other settings — the home, the learning laboratory, the psychiatric interview — while they may present us with ideas about how we might change our classroom teaching, cannot simply be transferred from one

*Just how different has been explored to some extent by Philip Jackson (*Life in Classrooms*, chapter 1).

setting to another without reference to context.

From your own experience you will be aware by now that classrooms have cultures of their own, and you may even have felt yourself becoming one person in the classroom and another outside it. For some people this can be quite a shock — similar to the 'cultural shock' anthropologists have reported when they have tried to live in a foreign culture. Whatever kind of analysis of profiles we attempt it must retain this fact as one of its major elements.

Returning to the problem of 'attracting the attention of the class' we can see that this is not a simple trick, or merely a question of learning a few standard techniques that will 'control' the class. (If you do believe this, and you find the 'tricks' won't work, you will come to believe that is because you have failed personally — that you 'will never make a teacher', that you lack some essential personality requirement.) In fact 'getting the attention of the class', as Kounin's research shows, can only be seen as part of a wider problem concerning management techniques generally. It is easy for a beginning teacher to overestimate the importance of being able to 'get attention' and for it to become an end in itself particularly as he/she may feel that this is what he/she is being judged on by other teachers, the children and college tutors.

One student teacher we observed in a biology class seemed to have no problems at the start of the lesson in transmitting various information and details of the experiment. Later, still standing in front of the teacher's bench, she exchanged questions about the work to be done. The 12—13 year old girls were extremely co-operative. They seemed not only to answer the questions satisfactorily but actually to rephrase the student teacher's questions for her — saying 'do you mean . . .?'. When they started the practical work the pupils seemed to be able to suggest both experimental method and presentation more explicitly than the teacher. By this time we began to realize (and this was confirmed by the recording) that her apparently effortless creation and direct sustaining of the initial part of the lesson was actually performed by and sustained by the pupils 'feeding' the teacher with cues and clues to the lesson structure. The end of the lesson — still impressively in control — involved questions about the experiment often reformulated and punctuated by the pupils, and repeated by the teacher from the 'front' out to the pupils. This student had all the superficial attributes of a teacher in a formal situation: stance, voice, and talk control.

Here was a teacher who had learnt more than the 'tricks'; she had succeeded in collecting and integrating much of the surface behaviour teachers use, but somehow failed to connect this up to create any effective communication. She had developed a certain 'style' and the girls in the class recognized this and played to it. There was, in fact, collusion between her and the class to make her appear an effective teacher. She was being the kind of person she thought a teacher should be, and not the kind of person she really was. She was dominated by what she took to be the 'role of the teacher'.

When we talk about 'role' we do not intend to specify the totality of what a person *is* in a situation. Instead we use the word to delineate the constraints on what a person can *be*.

We think it is useful to talk about two kinds of teacher performance within the classroom. One is the role involved in maintaining the attention of the whole class, for example talking to the whole class or managing a class discussion. The other is the role involved in transacting with one or two children, or a small group, say during a practical session. These two kinds of role performance we call 'teaching in formal situations' and 'teaching in informal situations' in

Varieties of formal situations.

order to underline the fact that they not only involve different kinds of role performance on the part of the teacher, but that they operate within quite different kinds of group structure. We want now to look at each of these aspects of the teacher's role in some detail.

Teaching in formal situations

What we want to describe here is the kind of performance that teachers give when they are 'whole-class teaching', when they have the whole class as an audience and are trying to direct attention to a common focus. Such situations are defined by the attempt by the teacher to monitor all utterances. In other words everything that is said in such situations is potentially public — everyone has access to what everyone else says. In such situations the teacher is usually highly visible and has to work to maintain the attention of the children. In other words the teacher can be seen to be doing two things: (1) maintaining the social context; keeping all the children included in the lesson, and (2) *using* this context to develop some idea, understanding or other piece of lesson content.

Sometimes these two tasks can be seen to interfere with each other — as when the teacher has to pause in mid-sentence in order to catch the attention of children who are not attending. Such hesitations may succeed in attracting their attention but may disrupt the logical flow of the utterance.

Example

T: What I want you to do now — (pause) — John. What I want you to do now is to try and write down what — (pause) — Will you boys at the back *listen* please (pause). I want you to write down what you have (pause) what you have just (pause) been doing.

Many teachers develop a repartee which they use to 'entertain' a whole-class group — salient gestures, jokes, characteristic phrases; and while for some this is a conscious performance that they take on and develop, for others it is quite unconscious. In all situations of this kind, however, it is common to find that the audience have more acute perceptions of the performance than the performer. Hence the success of college end-of-term skits in which the students mimic the teachers, and the ability of some schoolchildren to convey, at least to each other, the teaching persona of an individual teacher in a single phrase or gesture.

In studying teachers who are able to use formal contexts effectively it is often interesting to try and analyse their particular 'style'. This can be done by tape-recording lessons and transcribing bits that you feel are particularly effective. In this way try and get some idea of how they build up tension and release it — either by the use of question-answer sequences or by repetition and reiteration (this is a device used particularly effectively by some public speakers, as in Martin Luther King's 'I had a dream' speech). In both cases what is involved is a sense of sequencing and timing — both in the construction and delivery of individual phrases and in the way that these are linked together to form a structured sequence within which tension is built up and then released.

Consider the two following extracts, both from the same teacher and class, noticing how, even in transcript, there is still a real sense of the rhythm of talk:

Example

T: Now the question here is how many watt hours are the equivalent of three units? Three thousand watt hours. OK? Ten units . . .?

A: Ten thousand.

T: Ten thousand. Half a unit . . .?
Boys: Five hundred.
T: Five hundred. Good. Right (a) How many watt hours are equivalent to four kilowatts? Now what's a kilowatt?
B: Thousand watts.
T: A thousand watts. So four kilowatts will be . . .?
Boys: Four thousand watts.
T: Four thousand. Ten kilowatts . . .?
Boys: Ten thousand watts.
T: Quarter of a kilowatt . . .?
C: Two hundred and fifty.
T: How may units are required to supply a thousand watt fire for one hour?
Boys: One.
T: Ten hours . . .?
Boys: Ten.
T: Ten what . . .?
Boys: Units.
T: Two and a half hours . . .?
D: Two and a half units.
B: Two units five hundred watts.
T: OK, or two point five, fair enough. Half an hour . . .?
B: Five hundred watts.
T: Or point five. How many units are required to supply a two thousand watt fire for three hours?
B: Six units.
T: Six units. A hundred watt lamp for ten hours . . .?
Boys: One unit.
T: A five thousand watt iron for two and a half hours . . .?
B: Two units.
T: No.
Boys: One and a quarter units.

T: One and a quarter. Is it? You know how to work it out — five hundred times two and a half, over a thousand.

Example

T: The higher resistance you put in the path of an electric current the hotter it becomes. In an electric fire it becomes red hot — in a light bulb it becomes . . .?
A: White hot.
B: (Pause) Why doesn't it burn out then — in a light bulb?
T: What does *burn* mean?
B: Er, if it gets so hot . . .
T: What does *burning* mean?
B: Burning?
T: What does it mean?
B: Well. It's on fire.
T: What do you need in order that fire might come?
B: Oh! Oxygen.

Listening to teachers, and to tape recordings of their lessons you can frequently detect successful strategies that they repeat in different incidents, often playing complex variations on the same basic style. Here we give as an example, one attempt we have made to describe the style of a man we feel is a very effective teacher in formal situations. By listening to his lessons and going through recordings we have tried to extract what we think are the basic strategies underlying his 'style':

Jim Binham teaches a bottom stream fourth year class in a boys' secondary modern school. He has taught this particular class for about half their timetable throughout their four years at the school. His teaching style reflects the different settings in which he teaches. In the science lab, the greenhouse or the swimming baths he has an easy, informal relationship with individual boys, but in the classroom, where he teaches mainly English and maths, he relies heavily on whole-class teaching. Quite a lot of time in these lessons is taken up with discussion, arising from written work, from textbooks, or from pupil questions.

Listening to these discussions it seemed that there were two separate underlying qualities of control being used by the teacher. The first of these we call 'definition' — and use it to refer to the kind of role expected of the pupil during discussion. In highly defined situations the pupil is given a clear key with which to construct a response — there is usually a 'right' answer and a 'wrong' answer. Under low definition control the correct response is not nearly so clear, and the child has to create for himself a set of alternatives and then select an appropriate response, which may be one that is known only to himself.

Where 'definition' refers to the role system underlying verbal exchanges, a second kind of control relates to the logical sequencing of lesson content. Here we talk of content being 'open' when the pupil is involved in the negotiation of knowledge, or 'closed' when there are tight logical steps between one item and the next.

Distinguishing between two ways in which this teacher controls the topics and issues which are discussed — what we call high and low 'definition' and 'open' or 'closed' sequencing — gives us four kinds of talk strategy. The term 'definition' is intended to be analogous to 'definition' in the sense in which it is used in talking about an image on a televison screen or a piece of film — it refers to the extent to which the source produces 'fuzzy' or ambiguous information. It attempts to indicate the kind of knowledge an audience has to bring to the information in order to make sense of it.

'Open' and 'closed' sequencing is intended to reveal the kind of logic underlying the moves from one teacher utterance to another, and the degree of indeterminacy in that logic. Combining the concepts of 'definition' and 'content' we might expect to get a pattern like that in the diagram.

Teacher strategies for the management of knowledge

CONTENT OPEN
Utterances shift from general
to particular and from
objective to personal

COOK'S TOUR   FREEWHEELING

High definition ◄──────────► Low definition

FOCUSING

CONTENT CLOSED
Utterances shift from particular
to general and from
personal to objective

Examples of three of the categories, extracted from recordings made in Jim Binham's lessons, follow:

Focusing. In 'focusing' the teacher is converging on end-statements under high definition control. He knows the responses he wants the class to give.

T: Well anytime you taste sweat and tears, why does it seem to taste about the same level of saltiness? (pause) Blood. (pause) Well, think back to before we could think back. Before we were and were able to think.

A: Came from the sea.

T: Came where?

Boys: From the sea.

T: What came from the sea?

B: Fish.

T: All the . . . what?

Boys: Animals. Living things.

T: All living things as far as we know. And everything happened in . . . what?

B: In stages.

T: In stages yes. But everything happened, it happened in what?

Boys: In the sea. Evolution.

T: Yes, evolution originally happened in the sea. OK. So all life originated in what sort of environment, surroundings . . .?

B: Water.

T: What sort of water?

Boys: Salt, salty.

T: Salt water yes. In fact all the processes that go on in our bodies must go on in water. In . . . what's the word? Things in water . . . dissolved in water . . . all the reactions . . .?

C: Saturated.

T: Well, that's if you get too much.

D: Solution.

T: Yes, good. In solution. All the, you might say . . . chemical rearranging that goes on inside our bodies must take place in a salty solution, because when life as we understand it started, it started in what? . . . in a salty solution. OK? And our blood is salty, and must be kept at the same level of saltiness, so we believe, as the sea was when we started, where our forebears started. OK? This is why the blood doesn't get any more or less salty. If we have too little, when we sit down to dinner we somehow put a lot of salt on automatically, have you noticed this?

This example of focusing was only a part of a much longer sequence on the theme of the role of mineral salts in the diet of man. It illustrates several points. Notice the rejection of information: in one case where a boy suggests 'stages' the teacher wants the word 'sea', and in the other case where a boy suggests 'saturated' when the teacher wants 'solution'. Overall, definition is high, there is compression of knowledge through explanation, and moves from the personal and particular ('when *you* taste sweat and tears') to the objective and general. However, once the target is reached there is an immediate move back to the personal and particular (in the last sentence of the extract) which in fact signalled the start of a closed, high definition sequence.

Cook's tour. In the Cook's tour the teacher still knows the responses he wants the class to give, but instead of pursuing predetermined end-statements he shifts topics in an unpredictable fashion. This example is extracted from a lesson in which the class were checking some written English exercises:

T: Right, A., can you do the next one? (reading) Which month is said to come in like a lion and go out like lamb? And the second part, Which animal is supposed to behave madly or wildly in this month? Right A.?

A: The month is er March.

T: March, OK.

A: And the animal is er March hare.

T: March hare yes. Right do you know why?

B: Isn't it the er mating season?

T: Yes they — they all run around and show off to the doe; who's the female of the hare. Cartwheels and everything. I also believe that they chase each other and generally have fun, and it looks as though they've gone mad. If you've seen them you can approach to within touching distance, they just charge and charge around.

C: Oh yeah. (A noise of recognition)
T: Ah, is it, you know 'March winds, April showers, bring forth May flowers'. You've heard this? January's a cold month. What's February?
B: Second month of the year.
T: Yes. (pause) We talk about March winds, April showers, what's associated, in the north of England C.,* come on. (pause) Well, sometimes they talk of 'February fill-dyke'. What's a dyke?
D: A bank.
E: A ditch.
T: A water channel, a ditch. And February, in the north, I believe, is called February fill-dyke because this is the month when they get a lot of snow and rain, and all the water channels off into the dykes. In other words, it's a wet month. March winds — dry the ground — get the seed in. April showers, just enough to get these things growing, then May, the sun, and away we go. (pause). March hare. Go mad in March. Who can think of a story, or a character in a story —
F: *Alice in Wonderland*.
T: Who is supposed to be the March hare, and was a bit mad?
C: The Mad 'Atter.
T: The Mad Hatter, why the Mad Hatter?
C: Wore a 'at.
T: Yes, but why did they pick on the Hatter to be mad? Why not a mad tailor, or a mad cook?
F: Because hatters were meant to be mad.

*The teacher's personalizing of knowledge of C. with reference to the north of England is due to the fact that C. has recently come to London from Yorkshire.

B: 'Cause he made hats.
T: Well, at one time people who made hats used to use some chemicals which contained mercury. OK? Mercury is the stuff you get in thermometers, OK? This stuff is poisonous, and it would appear that after years of using this stuff it would get into their systems through their skin, maybe in powder form, I don't know, breathing it in. And this would affect, you might say, the way that their bodies worked, and they would go a bit potty. So anybody who had been a hatter for years was expected to be a little bit — funny — you know?

Here we have high definition control in the management of knowledge, with an overall logical structure of the open type. The teacher is guiding the class through disparate areas of knowledge under high definition control, pointing out features of interest along the way.

Freewheeling. In freewheeling the teacher allows the class to contribute in ways which *he* cannot predict, and the lesson takes on an open kind of sequencing.

T: Well, the people who have been investigating the later stages of pregnancy assure us that babies are aware. I mean, well, they don't hear people talking and so on, but they're able to sort of respond to a heart beat, they know if you stick a pin in them or something. I mean they move away from it, this sort of thing. They are as aware, say, a day before they are born, as they are a day after.
G: This bloke that lives up near me, he's gone deaf (noises of recognition) and he's a good bloke, but now he's gone deaf he sounds funny.
T: Yes (pause) there's a Member of Parliament who's suddenly gone deaf and he talks in a very peculiar way because he can't hear himself speaking. When you hear

yourself on recordings you always sound a little bit different from the way you think you do. The one way — sorry?

D: Mozart or someone.

T: No, Beethoven went deaf.

D: And he had to —

A: He sawed the legs of his piano off.

T: Well — (sceptically).

H: Yeah, he was sitting on a board wasn't he?

T: Yes?

C: Er . . . on the telly they was talking about the Apollo 10 and they was talking about something we got a middle ear or something. Have we?

Here there are no 'right' or 'wrong' answers, and the teacher is not immediately concerned with establishing some concept or set of facts, yet there are controls on the content of a subtle kind.

Educationally, an interesting question is how to get into the empty box in the diagram above . The obvious entry would seem to be via freewheeling, but clearly this is a process that presents considerable difficulties.

The labels we have used are deliberately rather jokey because what we want to emphasize here are not the categories we have derived, as end products worthy of deep study, but rather the process of trying to get under the surface behaviour to be observed in this classroom.

If you can find a teacher who you feel is particularly effective in formal contexts try and find ways of describing his/her performances. You may need to use recordings to do this and to collect quite detailed descriptions of particular incidents. This involves quite a lot of work but it can be very useful.

Teaching in informal situations

Here, we are talking about teacher performance when the teacher interacts only with one, or a few, children at a time. The teacher monitors some of the utterances; he is willing to 'not know' what is happening all over the classroom. It is a situation that is indeterminate both for teacher and pupils. Although for many students this seems a more 'natural' relationship it is also true that it demands considerable skill to practise. Not only is this kind of relationship more difficult to sustain than many people realize, but it also demands that the teacher is able to maintain an overall situation within which such relationships are viable. This second point is crucial. It is very rarely that a teacher can maintain 'informal' situations in schools where most teaching is formal. There are schools where individual teachers have managed to create a special climate in their own classes unlike that in other classes in the school. For example, some teachers can do this with remedial or low stream classes. In general, though, a stable informal situation in a classroom depends to some extent on the mood or climate in the school as a whole. In some schools it seems that the children themselves simply cannot handle the kinds of relationship that such situations demand. Consider this example from a junior school class:

. . . My first lessons in maths with 4C were occasions for clutching at the relative peace and quiet 'sums' seemed to offer. Adding up and taking away columns of figures seemed to appeal to them once they settled to it. . . . The maths problem was, and is, just part of the greater problem of the education of difficult children. The essence of the task is to get them to so organize their abilities and knowledge that they are put in a position where they can begin to be able to cope with a situation in which learning is demanded of them. . . . Although mathematically they are so inadequate

and today seem so indefensible, to us, sums gave minutes of
quietness and concentration and stillness, time to recuperate
lost tempers, theirs and mine, and to prepare for whatever
stresses and strains would come next. To be active in our
work, to learn from doing things in a room where others
were doing different things demanded too much from these
socially handicapped children. Doing mathematically
meaningless sums was for this class at this point of time
educationally more relevant than would have been any
attempt to go full-steam ahead in the direction of a
programme designed to help children to discover meaning in
mathematics.

Research Committee of the Institute and
Faculty of Education (1967) . . . *And
Softly Teach*, Achievements in Teaching,
No. 3 (University of Newcastle-upon-
Tyne), pp. 37—40.

We are not trying to argue that **formal and informal**
situations are inherently **good or bad** — they simply **make**
possible relationships which have **different qualities and**
different strengths.

Here it seems is a **teacher who would** (for himself) like the
class to be working predominantly within **informal**
situations — at least in maths, but who is **able to recognize**
the kinds of demands this makes on the children. He cannot
impose what he wants but has **to work for it by protecting**
the children's vulnerability.

51

Varieties of informal situations

When we talk about an 'informal situation' we are describing situations where groups of children, or individuals, are often working at separate tasks, and where the teacher moves round from group to group.

In the formal situation the attention of the whole class was on the teacher, and the attention of the teacher on the whole class. But in informal situations the attention of both teacher and child is more closely focused on the other.

Sequence: formal situation

From an hour-long formal session with a large group (70+ girls) at the beginning
of a new theme on the concept of 'historical period'. The teachers have brought
in various objects and pieces of music and are asking the girls to place them in
historical context. Notice how the focus of attention fluctuates from the objects
to discussion within this segment of the group. The situation illustrates the
knife edge which separates formal from informal contexts of classroom talk.

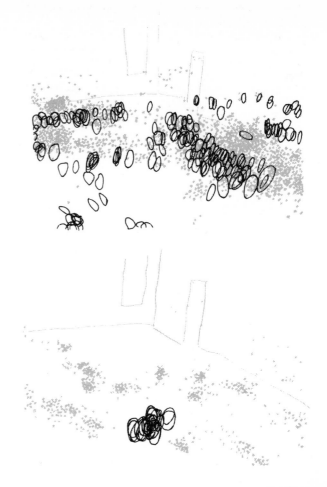

These three drawings attempt to reveal a structure of events in an informally organized classroom. Each drawing represents a period of fifteen minutes, the first from the beginning, the second from the middle and the third from near the end of a half-day session in an art class.

In each drawing the dots represent pupils and the circles the teacher. In the first drawing the pupils enter the room and after talking to the teacher establish themselves in work groups around the room.

In the second drawing the teacher deals with problems and travels from group to group encouraging and checking progress. In the third drawing the class sit in a circle and discuss their work during the session.

These drawings reveal that what may seem random and unstructured moment-by-moment may have a structure when viewed cumulatively over a period of time.

This kind of situation is most common in lessons that involve a high degree of practical work — science, art, craft, etc., and considerable skill in the management of resources. It is, though, a form of classroom organization that is becoming more common throughout schools.

Consider the following transcript which reveals a science teacher at work in such a situation. The way this transcript is set out may seem to make it difficult to decipher — but this is intentional. Setting it out as 'play-script' seems to distort the form of the talk. We have deliberately chosen a form of display that seems to us appropriate to the recording. Some visual context for the talk is given in diagram — where the last part of the sequence is illustrated with line drawings taken from film.

EXTRACT FROM COLIN'S SCIENCE LESSON
(The numbers in brackets are pauses in seconds.)

Now Benny (1.4) Now look (0.8) Take it off (1.6) See one (0.4) Two — three isn't it?

Oh (1.0) drastic.

Now then — is this nice and warm do you think? (1.2) Warm enough I should think (1.2). *Now* start adding some of this
Yeah.
to it (0.8) What are you going to lift it up on? (0.8) Microscope slide'll probably do — won't it?

(3.8) What' you doing?

(0.6) Adding this to it.

(1.4) All of it?

Not all of it, no — shake it up — see if it's going to dissolve easily (1.6) You've seen the instructions up there on what to do have you?

(0.4) Yeah —

You'll need your microscope again now won't you then? (1.6) Now — look —is that your microscope there?

Yeah.

Well you can set that up and have a good look at things (1.2) Has that dissolved all right — Yes let's put some more in it (2.4)

Can I do it now?

(0.4) Here you are. But set your microscope up because you'll need it in a minute (0.2) Now when it stops dissolving
Yeah.
(1.4) then stop adding any more (1.0) — set up the
Mm,   Mm,
microscope (1.2) Do as it tells you there in six — OK? (0.4) Yes Pete.

Er (1.8)

You've forgotten what you wanted?

That wood — you know — where — piece of paper where you light the bunsen burner.

(3.6) (sigh) Oh Jim (2.0) I don't know. What did you want — a piece of paper?

No — to light the bunsen burner.

You mean a splint?

— splint.

Ask Judy for one. Use your fingers! (0.8) . . . if it gets too
Colin
hot it means you're heating it too hard. (1.4) That's all (7.0) crushed it to a powder . . .
Colin.

That's fine

Can we have our . . . back?
No they can't can they?

No you don't need it (1.4) You only need a times four to start with.
See

    Look — all we can see is that great big fat lump.

Well — why — what's that doing there?

    (0.8) I don't know.
    Well it's — it's sort of —

—hasn't dissolved has it?

    No.
    . . .

Let's — let's take some of the stuff that hasn't got lumps in it.

    (0.6) Gail's.
    Colin.

(1.0) Get rid of that

    (0.4) Yes get rid of it Jane.
    We can't even see anything.
    Aren't we clever at science?

Well perhaps there's nothing to see yet.

    Aren't we — aren't we clever at science Colin?

Not very no.

    Ooh!

(1.8) Now then what have we got to do — you've got to *look* at this as it cools down.

    We can't even see the lump on it.

There shouldn't be —

    There's not supposed to be a lump.

There shouldn't be a lump should there?

    . . . you can't see it.

    Gail — the only fat lump we can see is you! (laugh)

Don't be rude.

    Don't be horrible.

Now you should be able to see now the liquid no crystals are forming . . . let it cool down — if *nothing* forms (0.8) Jane

    Yes.

If *nothing* forms as it cools down (0.6) heat it up again —

    And add some more.

— add some more

    . . .

No they won't — quite right . . . that for next time (0.6) Now, what's wrong with your? (4.8) Well it's far too bright really (1.0) Let's change the mirror a bit (3.0).

    What thingy — lens are we supposed to have it on Colin?

(2.0) Times four — to start with. This is all rattling isn't it?

    All this —
    Yeah.
    Yeah.
    It's the whole table.
    — table.
    It's not it's that.
    — smallest —

Yes — the smallest end that's right (3.0)

    . . . number four might be the biggest.

(0.4) No that's nine times twenty (1.2) Now — if you can manage to stop it wobbling for a minute (1.6) You're looking now at the surface of the liquid (1.6)

    . . . looking at my chemistry thing — I found it in the bin over there.

(1.6) Well it's not any good to us (8.0)

    Now?

Yeah I think we should bring this to the end of doing these now Pete — make this the last thing you look at and draw — all right?

    (0.4) Got a match?

(1.4) I haven't got one — but if you ask (0.4) Julie I think she's still got a splint to light things with (0.8) *What* is going on here? (2.6) Why is there smoke coming out of there Benny? (2.2) And what's this doing there? (2.0) What were you using it for?

    (0.8) Eh?

(1.0) What were you using it for?

    (1.0) Stop that thing!

(0.8) Ah — to do what — to light it . . . you got . . .

    It keeps bubbling!

. . . If it's bubbling you're heating it too hard (0.8) That's all (1.8) All you've got to do is turn it down lower.

    (0.4) Lower?

(0.8) Now *that* goes in a bin — go and put it in one — go on (1.0) There's one over there (5.8) What must there be under that asbes — that bunsen burner?

    (1.0) Asbestos.

Good lad.

    It's not working — shall we heat it up again?
    Ours hasn't worked yet.

Well if nothing's coming into it, add a bit more (1.0) in fact —

    This is ours.

That's yours is it?

    That one.
    Yes.

Well (2.0) perhaps it hasn't cooled down enough yet.

    We've got a crystal.
    Where?
    Look here! Have a look at it! Go on! Look!
    It's a — sand grain.
    — is it?

Yes (3.6) patience, patience Gail, that's all.

    (2.4) he's spilt it (1.0) He'll —
    — my book.
    — my 'and.

Well all right.

    — my 'and.

Well it won't hurt you — come — can you get back to it?

    Yeah.

Well why — what are you wandering round looking lost for?

    (0.6) I want a . . .

What for?

    Hold that with.

Hold it with your fingers.

    Oh! won't burn yourself.

First of all do it on a *cold* flame.

    (1.0) Yella.

Then if it gets too hot then you know you're heating it too much aren't you? (3.8) And if you hold it at a bit more of an angle (1.2) you'll do yourself less damage (1.0) Just point it away from your face.

    Crystals! Crystals!

Now don't get quite so excited Jane (2.0 um) Don't point it at David while you're heating it — it might shoot out into the eye (3.0) Let's have a look.

> Crystals!
> Colin, crystals!

All right Sandra, don't be so silly please (4.2) Where?

> (laugh)

(1.4) Where?

> There Colin!
> The shady bits.

(1.4) Nothing there (5.0) There's no crystals growing there yet (2.8) . . . There isn't any (1.8) The crystals haven't started to form yet.

> But what are *they* then?

They're just bits of dirt . . . at the bottom.

> (1.0) Shall we clean it?
> Oh dear.

No it's too late now.

> Oh Jane —

Just leave it to cool down.

> Right.
> (1.6) There's a little dot coming out.
> We haven't even got little dots.
> Yes we have!

You have — they're all over the place (3.8) Well it does say J — both of you in fact — written down on the sheet — that to make good crystals takes a lot of patience.

> (3.4) *Good* crystals?
> Which is one thing I haven't got.

Well you'll have to learn it won't you Karen.

We keep — we keep lighting our thing — and he keeps blowin' it out.

(1.4) Rob — yes (0.8) True or false? (3.6) Then stop being a bloomin' idiot will you please (2.0) Can I see what you've been doing so far? (5.2) Now, you didn't see all of that under a microscope —did you?

. . .

Well just show the bits you saw — under the microscope (1.2) I know what a two pence piece looks like (2.4) Not good enough Rob — sorry not impressed with this (0.6) You can do a *lot* better (1.0) Yes girls?

> Colin I can't get . . .

(10.0) Well what's that supposed to be love? (2.4) Well that's all — all lumps of copper sulphate in it aren't there?

(2.0) We're interested in the nice clear liquid here (1.2) all of you seem to have got lumps in this as well — haven't you? Look see? (1.4) See all those lumps there (1.8) It's nice clear stuff we want (0.8) Actually it's just on time to pack away — that's fine yeah — use that again (1.2) Right. *Listen* please HJ [the name of the class] (1.0) Listen please (3.8) All of you (2.0) As it's — it's quarter past — the last five minutes is clearing away time (1.2 em) those people who've *got* (1.0) some copper sulphate (1.0) solution (0.8) already made up (0.8) in there (0.6) We'll keep it until next time (0.6) If you could please stick a piece of paper in it (0.6) with your names on it (0.6) and bring it to me at the end of the lesson (0.4) I'll put it away in a locker (0.6) and you can collect it next time (1.0) Everything else please cleared away.

Total time of extract nine minutes.
Recorded February 1972.

60

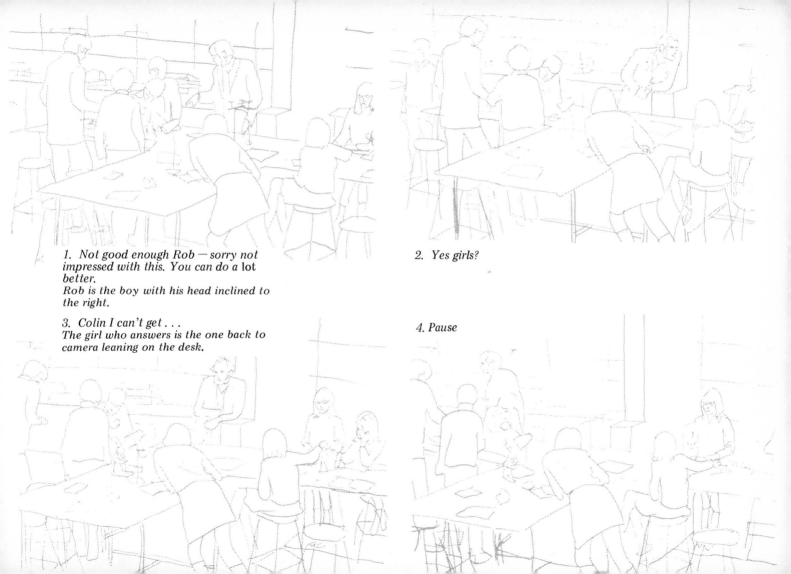

1. *Not good enough Rob — sorry not
impressed with this. You can do a lot
better.*
*Rob is the boy with his head inclined to
the right.*

2. *Yes girls?*

3. *Colin I can't get . . .*
*The girl who answers is the one back to
camera leaning on the desk.*

4. *Pause*

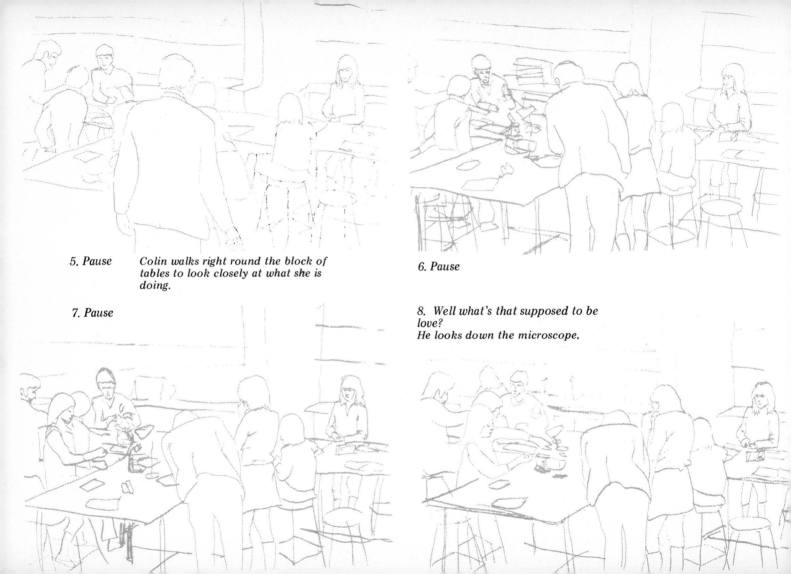

5. *Pause*   *Colin walks right round the block of tables to look closely at what she is doing.*

6. *Pause*

7. *Pause*

8. *Well what's that supposed to be love?*
He looks down the microscope.

9. Pause

10. Pause
She passes something to a friend (?)

11. *Well that's all — all lumps of copper sulphate in it aren't there?*

12. Pause

13. We're interested in the nice clear liquid here.

14. All of you seem to have got lumps in this as well — haven't you?

15. Look see. See all those lumps there? it's nice

16. — clear stuff we want
Notice how he stays hunched over to remain at the girl's height, and tends to talk to her face to face, (13) or to use the resources/task as a means of mediating the conversation (15/16)

17. *Actually it's just on time to pack
away.*
*He stands up and steps back — closing
the encounter.*

18. *That's fine yeah — use that again.*
Said to the next girl in the corner.

19.
*Moves away from that group into a
'neutral' location in order to make an
announcement.*

20. *Right* listen *please HJ.*

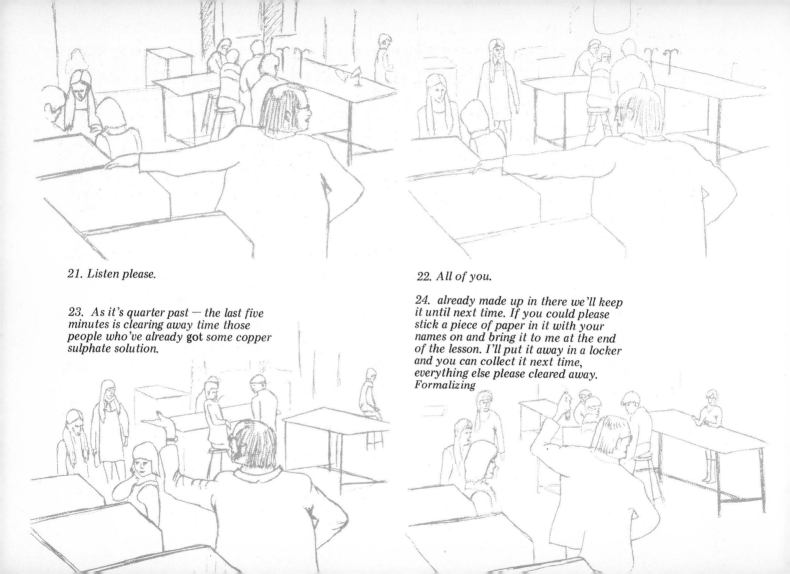

21. Listen please.

22. All of you.

23. As it's quarter past — the last five minutes is clearing away time those people who've already **got** some copper sulphate solution.

24. already made up in there we'll keep it until next time. If you could please stick a piece of paper in it with your names on and bring it to me at the end of the lesson. I'll put it away in a locker and you can collect it next time, everything else please cleared away. Formalizing

Informal sequence A

From transcript alone it is difficult in informal situations to tell who is talking to whom, and what is being talked about: switches in direction and topic are crucial to understanding what is being said. These photographs reveal rapid changes often marked by gesture, posture and facial expression.

Notice that talk involving personal responses to the situation is not suppressed by the teacher. This talk interpolates with the talk about the task. Until the last few seconds of this extract Colin is working within an informal situation, though at the end of the extract he formalizes the situation in order to orientate the children with new instructions. Compare the kind of talk being used here with the talk used in formal situations. It appears more fragmented and less continuous and in fact it is often impossible to understand without more information about the situation from which it was extracted. This is partly because a practical task is involved and as well as talking the teacher and children are also looking down microscopes, heating solutions, fetching and carrying equipment, and all this tends to interpolate the flow of the talk. The talk itself is also much less predictable — it is difficult to know what is going to happen next and the factors which determine what does happen are not always clear.

The point we want to make in comparing this extract with those from Jim Binham's class is *not* that one of these teachers is good and the other bad (we think that they are both extremely good) but that the contexts in which they are performing are quite different, and in particular the way in which talk is used in each situation is quite different. In the extracts from the formal situation talk is used in a very abstract, literary way to handle complex and difficult ideas: the exchanges resemble moves in a chess game. In the extract from Colin's lesson, talk is being used in a quite different fashion —it might *seem* awkward in transcript but in fact it is being used as a *process* rather than as an end product and so it can only really be understood when seen in its full context.

Maybe we can clarify this point by looking at one problem that faces the teacher in informal situations.

When the children are all working at different rates on a selection of tasks and the teacher moves around the class from group to group or from child to child, one the things that the teacher is constantly trying to do is to assess whereabouts each child has got to in his or her task. Where a clear artefact is involved (a dissection, a painting or drawing, a chemical experiment) it is easier for the teacher to operate than it is when the task is abstract. Notice in the extract from Colin's science lesson just how much of the talk is about physical objects of one kind or another.

In opening each fresh encounter with a child, or group of children, the teacher will have the task of 'plotting the co-ordinates'. When the tasks are such that the teacher cannot immediately tell what stage each child has reached, he has the problem, in each fresh encounter, of discovering a starting point from which both he and the child can begin talking without cross purposes. We call this recognition process 'plotting the co-ordinates' because the teacher usually has some plan in mind about the lesson, and is constantly fixing the locations of children on this outline in order to make sense of what they seem to be doing and to check their progress.

Here we give an example of a teacher trying to plot the co-ordinates of a child on his lesson outline. In this instance the child is actually off the map, and the teacher has to redefine the child's ideas about what constitutes a legitimate task in this lesson.

(Incidentally the teacher is Colin and the class is the same first year class as in the previous extract. The subject though is English-social studies, not science.)

Colin: What are you doing?

B: (1.0) I'm doing what's here.

Colin: (1.0) Why?

B: (1.0) I couldn't find anything else to do.

Colin: (1.0) Jones, occasionally you're a nit (1.2) More than

Informal sequence B: 'plotting co-ordinates'

The teacher has to be able to enter conversations at appropriate points, and often has to switch from one topic to another with some rapidity. Notice how the girl who is waiting to talk to the teacher gets into conversation with a friend.

occasionally (1.0) Let's have a look (3.4) Now when I last saw you, last week (0.8) you were carrying on some more work on Portugal for Madge weren't you?

B: (0.8) Yeah.

Colin: Is that right I've seen that haven't I (1.0) Now (1.4) What did you do with Madge then, on Friday and Monday?

B: (2.2) I did — I did this on Monday.

Colin: (0.4) What were you doing on Friday?

B: In here.

Colin: What same work (0.6) So you finished that stuff on Portugal you were doing for her —

B: No I just — I was having a break (1.6)

Colin: Well if you're having a break how about following up some of the work that, you know (1.8 um) Mary and (0.8) Gordon and Richard prepared for you?

B: Yeah.

Colin: There was a pretty good — a pretty fair amount of effort put into it by them (0.8) Yeah and you haven't done very much on them yet have you?

B: I've done something on theatre I done that plan (1.2)

Colin: Yeah.

B: . . . theatre (0.8)

Colin: Well (2.8) there's *something* here but I mean not an awful lot is there really (1.6) There's something on colour that was quite good (1.0) All right (2.0 um) I'm quite happy with you doing this (1.0) providing *it is just* a break (0.6) All right?

B: Yeah.

Colin: Don't lose sight of everything else (0.8) If it's just a

break, it's a lesson break, all right.

B: Yeah

Colin: So you know at the end, when I see you tomorrow (0.8) you'll have finished this (0.8) and (0.8) you'll be carrying on either with your work (0.2) quickly to finish off on Portugal or some more work on television and theatre (0.8)

B: Yeah.

Notice how Colin gets the boy to tell him what he is doing and, having pushed aside some veiled attempts at deception, gets to the truth that the boy is 'taking a break'. Then, instead of doing the predictable thing — 'What do you mean "taking a break" — you don't take breaks in my lesson — you come here to work' etc., he actually uses the 'excuse' by redefining it as a series of acceptable tasks. It is only towards the end of this sequence that Colin imposes his intonation and speech rhythm on the talk, and then it is clear that the transaction is closed.

Summary
Our assumption is that the lesson profile describes the underlying structure of events taking place during a lesson.

One of the most significant of these structural features is what we have called the 'situation' within which teacher and children interact. We distinguish two forms of situation — formal and informal — and suggest some of the differences between them. The most important distinction is a completely different use of talk in each context.

Typical proxemic phases during an encounter

1. *Teacher notices boy who has his hand up and walks towards him.*

2. *At a certain distance there is a mutual recognition of the encounter. The boy lowers his hand and the teacher asks what is wrong.*

3. *The teacher looks over the boy's shoulder at the task.*

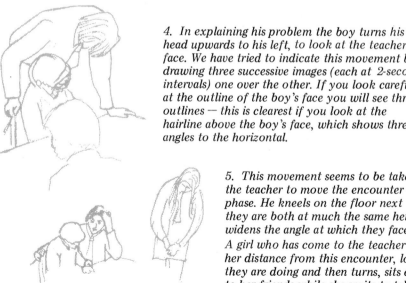

4. *In explaining his problem the boy turns his head upwards to his left, to look at the teacher's face. We have tried to indicate this movement by drawing three successive images (each at 2-second intervals) one over the other. If you look carefully at the outline of the boy's face you will see three outlines — this is clearest if you look at the hairline above the boy's face, which shows three angles to the horizontal.*

5. *This movement seems to be taken as a cue by the teacher to move the encounter into a different phase. He kneels on the floor next to the boy so they are both at much the same height, and he widens the angle at which they face each other.*
A girl who has come to the teacher for help keeps her distance from this encounter, looks at what they are doing and then turns, sits down and chats to her friends while she waits to talk to the teacher.

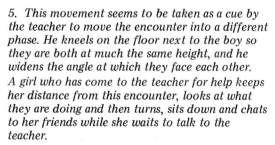

6. *The teacher stands and walks away, thus terminating the encounter.*

2. SEEKING THE TEACHER'S ATTENTION

Teachers often feel that the main barrier between the way they would like to teach and the way they actually teach is the fact that classrooms are so crowded. An overwhelming sensation for the beginning teacher is of being *rushed* — of never having time to establish the relationships or self-identities that they would like to establish (see for example the opening chapter of Bel Kaufmann's *Up the Down Staircase*).

Our approach here is to avoid taking as models for teaching relationships between adult and child those established out of school, whether in psychology labs, in psychiatric care or in the family. We have tried instead to look at actual classroom situations and to see what is possible within them.

A problem that immediately arises is how the children get the teacher's attention when they want help. We are not here talking about 'pleas for help' in the psychiatric sense, or the problems of communication involved within teacher-pupil relationships. We want to look quite simply at the constraints on interaction given the nature of teaching spaces and the sizes of groups within them. Classrooms are generally crowded places. Pupils take their turn, queues form, hands are raised, groups aggregate around the teacher. In all classrooms some means of scheduling and sequencing contact between teacher and pupils exists.

One characteristic of classrooms is that pupils seek teachers' attention at moments of doubt. The mediating variables constraining the seeking of attention include

1. shape of the room
2. distribution and dimensions of furniture
3. noise level
4. the number of people in the room and their distribution
5. age and type of group
6. type of activity
7. the social situation(s)
8. the expectations and norms of actions of the teacher, pupils and school.

Although most classrooms are rectangular, their proportions may be such as to prevent consistent effective eye-scan by the teacher.

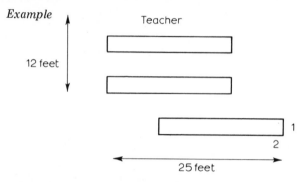

Example

A pupil with hand up at, say, site 1 or 2 may be missed by the teacher who is scanning mid-distance (approximately 12 feet), as many teachers tend to do. The fixed furniture may act to break up the room shape allowing seating arrangements that are difficult for the teacher to scan.

The raised hand is a culturally accepted signal for attention seeking in situations where the participants have quite rigid expected roles. However, it may have many *meanings*.

Just how complex the possible meanings of an apparently simple signal can be is well illustrated by the 'raised hand'. The photographs reveal a range of meanings, according to the context in which the action is performed. Some seem straightforward, others ambiguous, but it certainly is over-simplifying to treat the 'raised hand' as a simple signal of application to participate in the channels carrying public information within the social context of the classroom. Consider this analagous description of the meanings conveyed by another apparently ritualised signal — the military salute:

'During World War II, I became at first bemused, and later intrigued, by the repertoire of meanings which could be drawn upon by an experienced United States Army private and transmitted in accompaniment to a hand salute. The salute, a conventionalised movement of the right hand to the vicinity of the anterior portion of the cap or hat, could, without occasioning a court martial, be performed in a manner which could satisfy, please, or enrage the most demanding officer. By shifts in stance, facial expression, the velocity or duration of the movement of salutation, and even in the selection of inappropriate contexts for the act, the soldier could dignify, ridicule, demean, seduce, insult, or promote the recipient of the salute. By often almost imperceptible variations in the performance of the act, he could comment upon the bravery or cowardice of his enemy or ally, could signal his attitude toward army life or give a brief history of the virtuosity of the lady from whom he had recently arisen. I once watched a sergeant give a 3-second, brilliant criticism of English cooking in an elaborate inverted salute to a beef-and-kidney pie. It was

this order of *variability on a central theme* which stimulated one of the primary "breakthroughs" in the development of kinesics.'

Birdwhistell (1971) pp. 79—80

The raised hand is not just a signal of application to speak; for the style in which it is performed it can be used to communicate a whole range of feelings about the teacher, the lesson, the time of day, or other children.

Even if we consider those situations where hand raising *does* appear to be a ritualised signal for responding to a teacher's question, or attracting his attention in order to seek permission to speak, then closer study of the messages involved reveal a more complex communication system than exists at first sight.

Let us look at a simple model which begins, 'Teacher asks question' and continues:

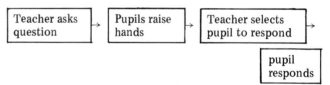

This kind of sequence would appear to form the basis of much teacher-pupil interaction during episodes of whole class teaching. If we look at this sequence in terms of the alternative options open to teacher and pupils we get a pattern something like that displayed in the diagram.

We stress again that this is a simplified model, a glance at the photographs emphasises this, yet even here the apparently simple sequence 'teacher asks question — pupil responds' as mediated by 'hands-up', conceals the possibility, for each child in the class, of eighteen different response strategies, and eighteen forms of non-response, each time the teacher asks a question.

Teacher Asks Question:

Pupil receives the message, although he may not understand it, or may understand it but be unable to answer.									Pupil fails to receive the message. He may not have been attending, or some noise source may have prevented him from receiving it.								
Pupil signals to teacher by raising hand, or some more subtle gesture. There may be some verbal or vocal signals.						Pupil does not signal to the teacher.			Pupil signals to teacher — perhaps in imitation of other pupils. The signal may be deliberately ambiguous (e.g. a half-raised hand).						Pupil does not signal to the teacher.		
Teacher receives pupil's signal. He may:			Teacher fails to receive pupil's signal						Teacher receives pupil's signal			Teacher fails to receive pupil's signal					
Signal to pupil to respond by gesture or utterance		No teacher signal	Teacher may still signal to pupil to respond		No teacher signal	Teacher asks pupil to respond		No teacher signal	Teacher signals to pupil to respond		No teacher signal	Teacher may still signal to teacher to respond		No teacher signal	Teacher asks pupil to respond		No teacher signal
Pupil receives teacher signal	Pupil fails to receive teacher signal		Pupil receives teacher signal	Pupil fails to receive teacher signal		Pupil receives teacher signal	Pupil fails to receive teacher signal		Pupil receives teacher signal	Pupil fails to receive teacher signal		Pupil receives teacher signal	Pupil fails to receive teacher signal		Pupil receives teacher signal	Pupil fails to receive teacher signal	
Pupil response / No response	Pupil response / No response	Pupil response / No response	Pupil response / No response	Pupil response / No response	Pupil response / No response	Pupil response / No response	Pupil response / No response	Pupil response / No response	Pupil response / No response	Pupil response / No response	Pupil response / No response	Pupil response / No response	Pupil response / No response	Pupil response / No response	Pupil response / No response	Pupil response / No response	Pupil response / No response

74

With the model in mind we can enter a fictional classroom and get some idea of how it works in practice:

Scene
The chemistry laboratory in a small, co-educational, rural Grammar School. It is the first lesson on a hot summer afternoon. Wearing a white lab coat, the teacher stands at one end of the lab, on the raised dais behind the demonstration bench, in front of the long blackboard. The class, who are in the first year, enter the lab, hot and excited from their lunch break, and find their way to stools around the practical benches.

T.   'Alright Class 1B. Settle down.' (Pause).

At this the class quietens, becomes suddenly lethargic, and turns to watch the teacher. He continues, in a rather brisk fashion that thinly disguises his own sense of lethargy.

T.   'Now remember, last week we all did an experiment. We had a series of test-tubes with different metals in them, and we added to these a solution. Now can someone tell me what this solution was?'

The children are clearly aware that a question has been asked, but there is a delay before they respond, during which time they observe the teacher very closely. Slowly, one child, a boy sitting near the front of the class (and probably on the left hand side), raises his hand. The teacher ignores this gesture, there is a further pause, and (rather sternly) he says:

T.   'Alright Class 1B. I know it's Friday afternoon, and I know you've all had syrup pudding for dinner, but this is a chemistry lesson and we have got some work to do.' (Pause. He visibly relaxes, his voice softens, and he continues). 'Now think back to last week. We had

several different metals. We put small bits of each into different test-tubes, and then we observed what happened. Come on Class 1B, think back to last week. What was the solution we used?'

By now three or four more hands are raised — mostly clustered around the boy in front, who is now propping up his arm with his other hand.

T.   'How about someone at the back?'

At this several hands near the front go up.

T.   'One of the girls?'

Several boys raise their hands.
     Now about a quarter of the class have their hands raised. A game ensues in which the children try to raise their hands when the teacher is not looking at them. It seems rather like that children's game where you must not step on the lines between paving stones — if the teacher catches you in the act of raising your hand you are out. At a critical point it is clear to the children that those who have their hands raised are *less* likely to be asked to respond than those who have not. At this point the game quickens and becomes more intense. As more and more children raise their hands, those whose hands are not raised appear more and more anxious — their eyes darting from child to child as the sea of raised hands closes in around them. Eventually the teacher selects a child whose hand is not raised.

T.   'Michael. Would you like to tell us the answer?'

Michael. (In some distress).   'Was it — was it, acid, Sir?'

T.   'Yes it was ACID. Does anyone remember what kind of acid?'

An obvious means of attracting the teacher's attention is the raised hand. But raised hands vary in the meanings they communicate, and have to be interpreted in context.

The boy who first raised his hand raises it again.

T.   'Yes John.'

John. (In a rather bored tone).   'Dilute hydrocloric acid, Sir.'

T.   'Yes John, quite right. It was dilute hydrocloric acid.'

He turns and writes it on the board. The children visibly relax.

Now we can see a further set of complexities, for, in terms of content, this sequence elaborates a single question, 'Which solution did we use last week?'. In the teacher's lesson plans all we would expect to see would be a minor note about recalling the work of the previous lesson. What we have tried to suggest is a set of different messages, carried largely through the 'hands-up' signal, within which apparently trivial comments ('I know you've all had syrup pudding for dinner')

have a significant function. We would suggest that episodes like this are basically about establishing a social structure and a set of relationships within which the teacher can teach in the way he intends. The significant messages in this situation are largely being carried through extra-verbal channels, and particularly through 'hands-up'.

Hand raising's main functions are

1. to signal that pupil has perceived that teacher is asking a question and that pupil is willing to try to answer it
2. to signal that pupil has interpreted a teacher utterance as one that may have concomitant questions
3. less often, that the pupil has appreciated for himself that a question is necessary because of some point to be clarified etc. This is usually the situation with older or communicatively competent pupils (in general or within the system of that subject in particular, including mathematics).

Getting the teacher's attention: sequence A

Pupils have to monitor the teacher's actions in order to
time their attempts to catch his attention.

(1) and (2) indicate that the pupil has appreciated that the
teacher is giving a space (transaction pause) for pupil talk.
However, transaction pauses and hesitation pauses may be
misinterpreted. If the teacher does not intend his utterance
to elicit a question, he may ignore the raised hand, or even
signal that the hand should be lowered. Where hand raising is
the only (legitimate) signal system for attracting attention,
indications of successful control include:

1. No shouts of 'Sir!' before the answers are vocalized
2. No leaving of seats

However hand raising may sometimes be observed to be a
ritual. For instance — before the teacher completes the
'sense' of a question children may have raised their hands. We
have noticed this especially in competitive situations —
eleven plus groups etc. If the context changes from
seatwork/listening/answering questions to, say, a practical
session, then the significance of the raised hand changes
meaning. In the practical a hand up may mean 'I need help'.
In the high definition situation the pupil waits until he gets
attention — i.e. he is seen. In the low definition situation
where roles arise in the course of spontaneous activity the
pupil may 'call out' — the teacher's name, the answer, or a
suggestion etc. Hand raising may still occur in conjunction
with these. It is worth noting if the pupil calls out more than
just the name of the teacher (i.e. just the summons). Usually
it is the summons that attracts attention. If the question or
answer itself is stated at 'public' distance (i.e. over 12 feet)
then, especially in a more physically active classroom, the
question becomes part of the noise. It is worth noting how
and at what instant of teacher's scan, posture and
relationships with other pupils' attention is sought.

Attention seeking: science lab

1. Teacher talking to P1a and P1. P2 is waiting for attention, having walked over from his own bench.

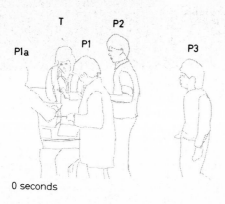

0 seconds

2. P3 enters angle between P1 and P2 and first catches teacher's eye at the close of her encounter with P1, P1a.

2 seconds

3. P2 steps back. T and P3 close and a new encounter begins with P2 again waiting.

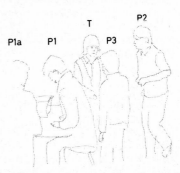

4 seconds

Getting the teacher's attention: sequence B

In an informal situation actions tend to become integrated into a network of responses and counter-responses. Here the girl in the striped sweater takes her book to the teacher, and while waiting for his attention she gets the comments and judgements of her friends.

Less frequent means of attention seeking include facial expression (participants have to be in eye contact at less than 12 feet — with good sight). This is mutual but teacher usually dominates with facial expressions 'Isn't that so?', or pupil 'I don't understand', or with accompanying hand signal 'come over here'. These signals are more subtle. In a large group, i.e. over fifteen, they are not usually effective. However, they are more intimate and specific than the raised hand for seeking attention.

Evidence from John Withall's research* indicates that even if a teacher is told that his contacts with some pupils are much fewer than with others, he can never, even though he tries compensating, spread his contacts evenly.

In an informal situation increase in the extent of doubt may arise because the task is too difficult, not well enough explained, the resources difficult to manipulate and locate etc. Eventually the demand for attention provides the teacher with a quite full means of monitoring the overall situation. Then, by default, the situation shifts from informal to formal.

3. TALK AND SILENCE

The main activity in the typical classroom is talk. The adult (teacher) has, in general, a greater facility with talk than the pupils. Talk is one of the major controllers of action available to the teacher. How the teacher uses talk reveals much about the situation under observation. From his research Ned Flanders has suggested a 'law': for two-thirds of the time in classrooms there is talk and of this time two-thirds is teacher talk. This 'law' arises from his studies of the seated-row-of-pupils-with-teacher-out-front situation of the typical (at the time of his research and to a large extent now) American school. The 'law' tends to be applicable in those settings and situations, but not in informal situations.

There are many aspects of control through talk — some of them are silent (e.g. distance from other people, angle of eye gaze, height, gestures and facial expressions). Those that may be heard usually include intonation, stress, volume, tone and pauses. Semantics (word meanings in context) and syntax (sentence structure) cannot be 'heard' but may be analysed

*John Withall, 'An objective measurement of a teacher's classroom interactions', *Journal of Educational Psychology*, 47 (1956), pp. 203—12.

Getting the teacher's attention: sequence C

An art class: the girls are preparing exhibitions for their CSE art exam. Teacher says, 'It was a period when I was looking at everybody's work to develop it for their CSE exhibition. J (the girl in the chair) was stuck. At the beginning of the lesson everyone wanted things and she had to wait for ten to fifteen minutes. C (the girl in the striped sweater) is always very demanding of the teacher's interest and attention.'

The prints being examined from frame 2 onwards are J's, but C remains within the circle of conversation and is later joined by a third and the Nigerian girl. Some of the discussion (frame 6) is about the texture of the silk screen used by J to produce the prints — she has spread glue over the screen.

(often only subsequent to the action). It is important that concern with these aspects of talk should always be related to their social context; only then may the semantics and syntax be appreciated as part of human communication.

Talk is action; it can control future developments and make sense of past actions. It can persuade people to perform actions. Talk is a powerful, sensitive yet fragile means of control. It can be interrupted. Talk is elusive. Subsequent attempts at recall are at best only partial. Some means of recording is necessary. Transcripts are always reductions of the varying contexts of the talk. They may leave out the gestural, intonational, pitch, volume and tonal concomitants. Yet although these features are so integral to human expression through talk, transcripts still contain enough detail for 'outsiders' to the original talk to make interpretations and 'sense' of what is being said. Those who are familiar with the particular culture and its teaching/learning milieu will be able to reconstruct more of the nuances and connotative aspects of the communication.

It is amazingly difficult to sustain distance from any talk that interests you. You tend finally to become immersed in the process of communication. If, however, the talk is of less concern to you it becomes easier to sustain sufficient monitoring to note aspects like

1. changes of speaker, including overlaps
2. changes of topic and issues within a topic
3. who changes topic etc.
4. who initiates new topics
5. length of silences
6. if people stay on a topic or tend to stray intentionally or unintentionally from it.

As a teacher is deeply involved in the process of communication it is very difficult for him to sustain a systematic registering of these aspects. This is another reason why the observer's role cannot be sustained at the same time as the teacher's role except by those who have first explored in an exhaustive manner as an observer. Even then self-monitoring — through the effect of one's actions on others — is diverted by the appreciation that one's actions (which include talk) have unintended consequences. In the 'Observation handbook' the example given of a teacher's own lesson profile is a vivid example of a teacher who is able to sustain this self-monitoring.

Initially and subsequently, especially in problem cases, a way into making talk open for inspection and reflection — making it 'opaque' rather than 'transparent' — is to study and discuss with other 'observers'.

A note on production of transcripts
Only in some formal situations can a verbatim script be produced — the talk situation may be one of 'verbal "ping-pong" ', slow enough even for longhand to be sufficient. Most situations have to be tape-recorded to collect something like the full talk. In formal situations a system of categories into which particular utterances are placed may be satisfactory for some purposes. We will deal with the problems inherent in recording talk and using category systems later.

Tape recording
In informal situations tape recording of some kind is essential. The extent to which a recording is satisfactory depends on the purposes for which it is to be used. For linguistic analysis, including features like intonation and false starts, a recording of the quality of a radio-transmitted outside broadcast news correspondent is needed. For a transcript of the content of talk a news correspondent speaking on a poor quality telephone line across the Atlantic

would suffice — although it is a strain on the transcriber's concentration.

We suggest that an adequate way to proceed with the task of transcription is to start and stop the tape at pauses, writing down the intervening content. Not only does this method tend to prevent the need to return to an earlier segment, but the sensitivity to speakers that the technique engenders brings the transcriber closer to the participants on the recording. Just as the participants have to perceive pauses to interrupt, interpolate or introduce changes of topic and speaker, and have to distinguish pauses for breath from hesitation pauses, transaction pauses and manipulation pauses, so does the transcriber.

Talk features

Listening to all sorts of talk induces one to consider how the participants communicate (see diagram of communication model. A commonsense observation is that people talk about what is of concern to them. They talk about a topic, or issues within a topic. As the speaker they often expect the next speaker to 'keep to the same subject'. They do not want others to 'go off the point', 'change the subject' etc. in ways they cannot follow. If the speaker does not mind if the topic is changed he will usually indicate this by pitch variation, combined with gestural concomitants.)

Even jokes often follow the same topic. In fact being able to tell a joke depends not only on the content of the joke but on sensitivity to the topic of previous jokes in the general social context. If participants regularly (to the observer) change topics without any indication of why, then we often name this sort of talk 'chat'. However, speakers of close acquaintance who share many experiences in common may use talk as embellishment to the shared understandings (a long-married couple, two priests, bus conductors, street market traders). In addition topics that have been predetermined often generate the phenomenon of talk as embellishment. Some television current affair discussions rely heavily on the chairman to make the topic changes explicitly.

In formal situations topics tend to be marked even to outsiders. Informal situations range from explicit marking of topics and issues to sharing of the same certainties. Often these two features are found in a small section of talk.

Here is a list of questions that a participant observer could reflect on. The observations related to these questions provide features for accompanying what we call a talk form. The transition from one talk form to another is also potentially observable.

We have dealt at some length with talk because we consider that recognition of range and varieties of topic, and legitimate and non-legitimate issues within topics, reveal much about the extent of negotiation. In conjunction with other observable aspects of classroom study, sufficient detail to make reasonable inferences and connections is provided.

Questions	Interview	Dialogue	Chat	Committee meeting	
Are these specified statuses?*	Yes	No	No	Yes	Predetermined rules
Is there a possibility of deviation from status?	No	Yes	Yes	No	Predetermined rules
Is there a possibility of change of status?	No	Yes	No	No	Predetermined rules
Who has the right of speaker selection?	Rank/status dependent	Rank/status independent	Rank/status independent	Rank/status dependent	Predetermined rules
				Rank/status dependent	Ad hoc rules**
Who has the right to select topic?	Rank/status dependent	Rank/status independent	Rank/status independent	Rank/status dependent	Predetermined rules
Who has the right to change topic or area in topic?	Rank/status independent	Rank/status independent	Rank/status independent	Rank/status dependent	Predetermined rules
Who has the right to define the register to be used?	Rank/status dependent	Rank/status independent	—	Rank/status dependent	Predetermined rules
			Rank/status independent		Ad hoc rules

*The term 'status' attempts to include differences between people's official functions. Thus in a debate there are first, second and floor speakers, each of whom had particular rights and obligations within the situation of the debate. However, the impact of what they say, the manner in which it is said and the deviation from the official rights and obligations allowed before an objection is mainly dependent on the extent to which the debaters as a whole consider that the persons of particular status should stay within what are construed by others to be the rules underlying actions within the debate.
**Ad hoc rules — an unforeseen contribution which others accept and may be taken up, e.g. heckling at a political meeting.

Questions	Interview	Dialogue	Chat	Committee meeting	
Who has the right to change the register?	Rank/status dependent	Rank/status independent		Rank/status dependent	Predetermined rules
			Rank/status independent		*Ad hoc* rules
Who formulates summaries of exchanges?	Rank/status dependent	Rank/status independent	Absent	Rank/status dependent	Predetermined rules
Who has the right to reformulate summaries?	Rank/status dependent	Rank/status independent	Absent	Rank/status dependent	Predetermined rules
				Rank/status independent	*Ad hoc* rules
Are appeals to authority intra or extra† to the speakers?	Both	Both	Intra	Intra	Predetermined rules
Who has the right to interrupt or interpolate?	Rank/status dependent	Rank/status independent	Rank/status independent	Rank/status independent	Predetermined rules
What is the nature of demonstration of agreement, approval, disagreement or disapproval?††	Muted	Demonstrative	Demonstrative	Demonstrative	Predetermined rules

†Intra refers to knowledge within the group members. Extra refers to people's ideas, books, etc. that are not within the group.
††Muted, demonstrative or absent.

Questions	Discussion	Debate	Quiz	Trial*	
Are there specified statuses?	No	Yes	Yes	Yes	Predetermined rules
Is there a possibility of deviation from status?	Yes	No	No	No	Predetermined rules
Is there a possibility of change of status?	Yes	No	No	No	Predetermined rules
Who has the right of speaker selection?	Rank/status independent	Rank/status dependent	Rank/status dependent	Rank/status dependent	Predetermined rules
Who has the right to select topic?	Rank/status independent	Rank/status dependent	Rank/status dependent	Rank/status dependent	Predetermined rules
		Rank/status independent		Rank/status independent	Ad hoc rules
Who has the right to change topic or area in topic?	Rank/status independent	Rank/status dependent	Rank/status dependent	Absent	Predetermined rules
Who has the right to define the register to be used?	Rank/status independent	Rank/status dependent	Rank/status dependent	Rank/status dependent	Predetermined rules
Who has the right to change the register?	—	Absent	Absent	Absent	Predetermined rules
	Rank/status independent				Ad hoc rules

*Trial — very similar to quiz! See *Alice in Wonderland.*

Questions	Discussion	Debate	Quiz	Trial*	
Who formulates summaries of exchanges?	Rank/status independent	Rank/status dependent	Rank/status dependent	Rank/status dependent	Predetermined rules
Who has the right to reformulate summaries?	Rank/status independent	Rank/status independent	Rank/status dependent	Rank/status dependent	Predetermined rules
Are appeals to authority intra or extra to the speakers?	Both	Both	Extra	Extra	Predetermined rules
Who has the right to interrupt or interpolate?	Rank/status independent	Rank/status dependent	Absent	Rank/status dependent	Predetermined rules
What is the nature of demonstration of agreement, approval, disagreement or disapproval?	Demonstrative	Demonstrative	Absent	Absent	Predetermined rules

Questions	Lecture	Seminar in England	Seminar in Germany	
Are there specified statuses?	Yes	Yes		Predetermined rules
Is there a possibility of deviation from status?	No	Yes		Predetermined rules
Is there a possibility of change of status?	No	Yes		Predetermined rules
Who has the right of speaker selection?	Absent	Rank/status independent	Rank/status dependent	Predetermined rules
Who has the right to select topic?	Rank/status dependent	Rank/status dependent		Predetermined rules
		Rank/status independent		*Ad hoc* rules
Who has the right to change topic or area of topic?	Rank/status dependent			Predetermined rules
		Rank/status independent	Rank/status dependent	*Ad hoc* rules
Who has the right to define the register to be used?	Rank/status dependent	Rank/status dependent		Predetermined rules
Who has the right to change the register?	Rank/status dependent	Rank/status dependent		Predetermined rules
Who formulates summaries of exchanges?	Absent	Rank/status independent		Predetermined rules

Questions	Lecture	Seminar in England	Seminar in Germany	
Who has the right to reformulate summaries?	Rank/status dependent			Predetermined rules
		Rank/status dependent		*Ad hoc* rules
Are appeals to authority intra or extra to the speakers?	Extra	Both		Predetermined rules
Who has the right to interrupt or interpolate?	Absent			Predetermined rules
		Rank/status independent	Rank/status dependent	*Ad hoc* rules
What is the strength of demonstration of agreement, approval, disagreement or disapproval?	Muted			Predetermined rules
		Demonstrative		*Ad hoc* rules

Questions	Focusing	Cook's tour	Freewheeling	
Are there specified statuses?	Yes	Yes	Yes	Predetermined rules
Is there a possibility of deviation from status?	No	No	Yes	Predetermined rules
Is there a possibility of change of status?	No	No	No	Predetermined rules

Questions	Focusing	Cook's tour	Freewheeling	
Who has the right of speaker selection?	Rank/status dependent	Rank/status dependent	Rank/status independent	Predetermined rules
Who has the right to select topic?	Rank/status dependent	Rank/status independent	Rank/status independent	Predetermined rules
Who has the right to change topic or area in topic?	Rank/status dependent	Rank/status dependent	Rank/status independent	Predetermined rules
Who has the right to define the register to be used?	Rank/status dependent	Rank/status dependent	Rank/status dependent	Predetermined rules
Who has the right to change the register?	Rank/status dependent		Rank/status independent	Predetermined rules
		Rank/status independent		Ad hoc rules
Who formulates summaries of exchanges?	Rank/status dependent	Rank/status dependent	Rank/status independent	Predetermined rules
Who has the right to reformulate summaries?	Absent	Rank/status dependent	Rank/status dependent	Predetermined rules
Are appeals to authority intra or extra to the speakers?	Extra	Both	Both	Predetermined rules
Who has the right to interrupt or interpolate?	Rank/status dependent	Rank/status independent	Rank/status independent	Predetermined rules
What is the nature of demonstration of agreement, approval, disagreement or disapproval?	Muted	Demonstrative	Muted to demonstrative	Predetermined rules

Selection of words and phrases in talk

We tend to hesitate (and thus be potentially interrupted or interpolated) when we reach a point in an utterance when we have a wide choice of

1. words to use to convey intended meaning
2. structures upon which to superimpose the words (syntax).

Example A
'Of course, the point of what he has just said is that (hesitation) linguistic competence does not emerge as linguistic performance.'

Example B
'Put . . . the red hat . . . on'
(But not 'Put the red . . . hat on'
or 'Put the . . . red hat on'.)

Example B (from an experiment by R. Brown and Bellugi)* illustrates that hesitation most frequently relates to sentence *structure*, i.e. the noun phrase 'the red hat' remains a unit. This aspect of talk tends to be true for adults as well.

Two other sites of hesitation may occur:**

1. at the selection of the commencement of an utterance (observe that we often rephrase)
2. after and before a clause.

Of course, the hesitation is relative to the complexity (for the individual) of the cognition involved. This means both that the expression of complex ideas has relatively longer hesitation pauses and that complex ideas transformed to simple language (as in much teaching) involve considerable

*'Three processes in the child's acquisition of syntax', *Harvard Educational Review*, 34 (1964).
**A hesitation pause may be defined as one more than 0.2 seconds or longer. One aspect of stammering is that the hesitations occur at the same sites as in 'normal' speech.

hesitation. Only rehearsed talk is free of marked hesitation. (In debate the most verbally able politicians become practised in pausing towards the end of statements, not in the expected places — it makes interruption difficult (the utterances are most often preconceived before the interview or public meeting).)

Although hesitation and pausing have different functions in talk (waiting for a reply, allowing a silence to make a point stand out, taking a breath), they may be confused (intentionally or not) or misinterpreted. Talk to another usually contains pauses for the other to respond (transaction pauses).

In many classrooms these pauses are allowed after teacher questions and the raised hand is the sign that a transaction pause has been appreciated, but if discussion is allowed by the teacher then the possibility of interruption because of misinterpretation of *hesitation* for *transaction* pauses is greater.

Example

P: Why does an egg have white?
T: I'm not telling you everything mate (1.0)
P: Why does an egg have white?
T: Well a little bit of thought — if you're rolling about in an egg —
P: Yeah.
T: and you didn't have any white there every so often you'd be going clang, clang, clang.
P: The stuff that moves it.
T: Yes it's sort of like a cushion . . . (teacher's hesitation) . . . to keep it.
    (pupil interprets as transaction pause)
P: But you said it's cause . . . (pupil hesitation) . . . they eat the yolk, well where's the baby —
    (teacher interprets as transaction pause)

91

T: The baby's sitting on top of the yolk there, if there was not white the yolk would be rolling all over the place. I'll give you one of your own.
Come on I'll — you can have one of your own.

The number and length of transaction pauses seem to be characteristic of classroom relationships. The control of talk is mediated by transaction pauses — assuming that vocabulary and syntax are mutually comprehensible.*

It seems that the frequency and duration of transaction pauses in discussion (not so in teacher's questions to the whole class) is a manifestation of the more 'open', low definition learning situation.

In the more traditional setting the pauses are of the hesitation and transaction type. In most cases there is a clear mutual understanding of which is which — i.e. there is little possibility for misinterpretation or multiple interpretation (see function of raised hand again). The pauses relate to the grammatical structure. They often emphasize the knowledge sense of the utterances. The rather ritual repetition of a pattern of actions is manifested in the talk. The 'unexpected' event is clearly appreciated as deviant. It may be amusing or may provoke penalties.

In more 'open' situations the task often involves an element of autonomous pupil inquiry. In these cases manipulation pauses as well as the other two may break up the grammatical structure. The talk tends to get fragmented, interpolated within and by the activity, and by the particular children involved. With some idea of the significance of context in interpreting talk, and of the nature of hesitations in relation to the task, to movement around the room and to changes in the nature of the situation, we can perhaps begin to interpret the sequence from Colin's science lesson more

*'Slow' talk is not related to rate of speech but to length of hesitations.

fully. Look at this extract and try to relate the talk and pauses to the tasks.

(0.4) Got a match?

(1.4) I haven't got one — but if you ask (0.4) Julie I think she's still got a splint to light things with (0.8) *What* is going on here? (2.6) Why is there smoke coming out of there Benny? (2.2) And what's this doing there? (2.0) What were you using it for?

(0.8) Eh?

(1.0) What were you using it for?

(1.0) Stop that thing!

(0.8) Ah — to do what — to light it . . . you got . . .

It keeps bubbling!

. . . If it's bubbling you're heating it too hard (0.8) That's all (1.8) All you've got to do is turn it down lower.

(0.4) Lower?

(0.8) Now *that* goes in a bin — go and put it in one — go on (1.0) There's one over there (5.8) What must be under that asbes — that bunsen burner?

(1.0) Asbestos

Good lad.

It's not working — shall we heat it up again?
Ours hasn't worked yet.

Well if nothing's coming into it, add a bit more (1.0) in fact —

This is ours.

That's yours is it?

That one.
Yes.

Well (2.0) perhaps it hasn't cooled down enough yet.

    We've got a crystal.
    Where?
    Look here! Have a look at it! Go on! Look!
    It's a — sand grain.
    — is it?
Yes (3.6) patience, patience Gail, that's all.

    (2.4) He's spilt it (1.0) He'll —
    — my book.
    — my 'and.
Well all right . . .

    — my 'and.
Well it won't hurt you come — can you get back to it.

    Yeah.
Well why — what are you wandering round looking lost for?

    (0.6) I want a . . .
What for?

    Hold that with.

Words spoken: approval (from C. H. and C. K. Madsen,
Teaching Discipline (Alleyn and Bacon, 1970)

Words

Yes	Correct
Good	Excellent
Nice	That's right
OK	Perfect
Great	Satisfactory
Fascinating	How true
Charming	Absolutely right

Commendable	Keep going
Delightful	How beautiful!
Brilliant	Wonderful job!
Uh-Uh	Fantastic!
Positively!	Terrific!
Go ahead	Beautiful work
Yeah!	Marvellous!
All right	Exciting!
Exactly	Pleasant
Of course	Delicious
Likable	Fabulous!
Wonderful	Splendid
Outstanding work	Thinking
Of course!	

Sentences
That's clever
I'm pleased
Thank you
I'm glad you're here
You make us happy
That shows thought
We think a lot of you
That's good work
Remarkably well done
That shows a great deal of work
Yes, I think you should continue
A good way of putting it
I like the way . . . . explained it
That is a feather in your cap
You are very friendly
That's an excellent goal
Nice speaking voice
That's a nice expression

It is a pleasure having you as a student
That's interesting
You make being a teacher very worthwhile
That's sweet of you
Well thought out
Show us how
You're doing better
You are improving
You're doing fine
You perform very well, ...
That's very good, ...
I'm so proud of you
I like that
This is the best yet
That's the correct way
That's very choice
You do so well
You're polite
Thinking!

Expressions: approval
Facial

Looking	Widening eyes
Smiling	Wrinkling nose
Winking	Blinking rapidly
Nodding	Giggling
Grinning	Whistling
Raising eyebrows	Cheering
Forming kiss	Licking lips
Opening eyes	Smacking lips
Slowly closing eyes	Pressing lips affirmatively
Laughing (happy)	Rolling eyes enthusiastically
Chuckling	

Bodily

Clapping hands	Grabbing
Raising arms	Bouncing
Shaking fist	Dancing
Signalling OK	Stroking motions
Cocking head	Opening hands
Skipping	Flipping head
Rubbing stomach	Taking a fast breath
Thumbs up	Expansive movements of hands
Shaking head	Hugging self
Jumping up and down	
Shrugging shoulders	

Circling hand through air (encouragement to continue)
Hand/finger to face, eyebrows, eyes, nose, ears, mouth, cheek, lips, hair, forehead

Words spoken: disapproval
Impractical
Be prompt
Work faster
Try to understand
Do your homework
Do your best
Unclear explanation
Don't you want to do things right?
It can't be that difficult
You're too slow
Stop talking
Behave
Pay attention
Don't
Wrong
Stupid
Be still
Follow directions

94

Think for a change
Use some thought
No, that's not what I said
You don't understand because you don't listen!
If I find you chewing gum once more, you'll wear it on your nose
Be quiet and sit down
That's ridiculous
Meaningless
Absurd
Bad
Nonsense
Too vague
Try harder
Wrong
That's not right
Incorrect
Needs improving
Unsatisfactory
Poor
Undesirable
You should be ashamed
Useless
That's not clear
I dislike that
Don't be silly
That's terrible
What is this?
Is this something?
Let's throw this away
I can't read anything you write
Haven't you learned how to spell?
Grow up
You're not doing as well as you used to
Horrible

Absolutely not!
Shh!
Stop
Listen to me
Maddening
Be quiet
Raise your hand
Stop that laughing
I'll have no more talking
Apologize now
Sloppy
Shut up!
I'll show you who's boss
One more time and you'll get it from me
Finish it now
No talking
I'll slap you silly
Look for the answer
Leave her alone
You march straight to the office
Keep your eyes on your own paper
You lack interest
I'll give you something to cry about
You *couldn't* have done worse
I do not like this
It's not up to requirements
I will not repeat it
I'm not telling you again
You're dull
That's ugly
You idiot
You're a laughing stock
It's hopeless for you
You're cheap
Snob

You're worthless
You're rude
You're disgusting
You little monster
Don't laugh at me
Cut it out
You're filthy
You naughty boy
Mock me and you won't hear the end of it
You're narrow-minded
That's childish
Simple Simon
No! No!! No!!!
You haven't applied yourself
Your work isn't acceptable
Get your mother to sign this bad paper
What do you mean you're not finished?
Stand up straight
Just try that once more
Anyone else!
Learn that!
You'd better get on the stick
Speak when you're spoken to
Smart alec
You *must* be confused
I don't see your point
You know what happened the last time you did that
You do this over
You know better than that
Play fair
Don't cause problems
You're never dependable
That wasn't the right thing to do
Well, we'll never do this again
If you had a brain in your head, you wouldn't say that

Do it!
You think you're the only one here?
You're bad
Poor stupid oaf
Wrong again
You're doomed to failure
You're wrong all the time
You don't know anything
You make me sick
You're just an inadequate person
Impertinent
You're not thinking
You haven't been paying attention
Wipe that silly grin off your face
I guess I shouldn't expect any more from *you*
You're just plain boring
Terrible! Terrible!
This isn't what *I* had in mind
You know that's wrong
Stupid nonsense
You'd *better* try harder
People never change.

Expressions: disapproval

Frowning	Starting
Curling lip	Wrinkling forehead
Lifting eyebrows	Nose in air
Looking at ceiling	Puckering lips
Furrowing brows	Wrinkling nose
Smirking	Pounding fists on table
Lowering eyebrows	Laughing
Shaking finger or fist	Shaking head
Wrinkling mouth	Turning away
Squinting eyes	Gritting teeth
Biting lips	Twisting side of mouth

Squinting eyebrows
Looking sideways
Closing eyes
Clicking tongue
Pushing mouth to one side
Pointing finger
Putting hand behind ear
Grimacing
Sniffing
Tightening jaw
Sticking out tongue

Cackling
Snickering
Turning head away
Letting out breath
Raising lips
Hissing
Fingers in front of lips
Nodding head (no)
Showing teeth
Pulling in bottom lip

Section 2. Action

In the previous section we set out some ways in which lesson profiles, and the accounts and case study material collected to give them context, can be approached analytically. Although the lines of inquiry we have suggested are far from exhausted we have deliberately attempted to carry the analysis to stages which are beyond what most teachers will require: it is up to each reader to take the analysis as far as is useful for him, and if necessary to extend it further.

In this section we want to attempt a different use for the observational material — one which emphasizes the feeling of personal discovery rather than the style of an objective research inquiry.

As in the previous section what we have written is not intended to be in any way definitive. We want simply to present ideas and tentative experience. Our hope is that they will be an inspiration for action rather than debate. We want, briefly, to make the context of these ideas a little clearer, in the hope it might help others to relate them to their own situations.

STUDY GROUPS

In 1968—9 Chelsea College of Science and Technology began offering a one-year professional teaching course for science (and later mathematics) graduates at the newly established Centre for Science Education. The overall director of this course from 1968 to 1973 was Harold Silver, an educational historian. Many of the science staff at the centre were (or had been) involved in the Nuffield Science Teaching Projects, and so the one-year course had from the start a strong commitment to learning science through experimental investigation. Under Harold Silver's influence the social science elements of the course came to pursue a similar philosophy. Lectures were reduced to a minimum and were predominantly multi- or inter-disciplinary and the two main activities in the social science parts of the course became a written dissertation and participation in 'study groups'.

The study groups were intended to act as a central focus for the whole course. Each student was a member of two groups and each group met once a week for a full half day. Group sizes varied from eight to twelve students with one (sometimes two) staff members. The intention was that each group should construct its own curriculum; that staff were present as facilitators rather than as lecturers; and that none of the work of the groups was available for assessment. In practice, groups varied enormously in the way they worked and the things they did.

Nearly all the ideas and activities we have described in this book derive from the work of study groups we ran in 1971—2 and 1972—3 (one of us also having tried running groups in 1969—70 and 1970—1 in a much less structured manner).

It is important to emphasize that we have worked out these ideas in a context that emphasizes student autonomy, the validity of group experience and the fallibility of tutors, and one that is free from assessment. This within a total course that minimized disciplinary autonomy (in the social sciences at least) and put its main emphasis on active student learning rather than on thorough academic teaching.

The intention we brought to the study groups was to relate the activities of the group as strongly as possible to the immediate problems of teaching and of becoming a teacher. We tried to create non-threatening situations where students could rehearse newly discovered aspects of themselves. We wanted them to feel free to fail because we had a context where failure was not cumulative or self-damaging. We saw our role as primarily one of creating situations in response to expressed or perceived needs within the group. So we departed somewhat from the study group tradition; we took on responsibility for the curriculum (albeit that decision was often negotiated). We did this because we wanted the group to face squarely particular issues relating to teaching, and did not want to risk taking a chance on these emerging. Each of the students in the group did of course attend an alternative study group parallel with ours.

Discussing teaching with the group before and after first teaching practice seemed to reveal changes in the strength, specificity and orientation of their concerns during the experience. Some students, however, did not show any marked change in the urgency or commitment with which they related to the concerns of the group. Often these were students who had been sent on teaching practice to schools very similar to those they had attended themselves (usually direct grant grammar or public schools). Sometimes initial visits to such schools created strong feelings of rejection or animosity. It appeared they had rejected school themselves during their late teens and consciously reacted against their felt identity as 'school products'.

First teaching practice (which at Chelsea lasted about three weeks and took place after a short induction course in college) seemed to raise strong feeling around distinctions and parallels between the students' own school experience and what they felt about becoming teachers. Above all it crystallized around authority relationships, and (for these science and mathematics students) subject stereotypes and loyalties.

It seemed to us that first teaching practice could offer a profound challenge to identity, and that the sort of images of teaching that are usually presented to students at this point, both by colleges and by schools, they often find impossible to sustain in the classroom because the deeper conflicts remain unrecognized.

The problem we confronted was of trying to do something practically helpful for classroom teachers but which did recognize some of the deeper problems and issues. On the other hand we did not want to pursue the deeper issues to the exclusion of professional technique. The idea of approaching problems through counselling or activities like teaching groups seemed interesting but somewhat lacking in immediate concern. We did not want to run groups which were apparently only concerned with the group itself; we wanted the main concern to be directly with problems of teaching. To give some idea how we approached this ideal we want to describe two activities we devised, both of which are adaptations of orthodox techniques but drastically modified for our purpose.

MINI-TEACHING
Mini-teaching grew from our reading of experiments in the USA with microteaching and discussions with people who had tried such techniques in their own courses.* The ideas of microteaching — of playing back to students a recording of themselves teaching in limited and controlled conditions in

*Particularly Peter Fensham (Monash University), visiting professor at the Centre for Science Education 1970—1.

ways that allowed them the opportunity to attempt alternative strategies and to assess their success — seemed attractive. Our research, however, led us to reject the kind of analysis of skills used at Stanford in the original microteaching programmes and duplicated in many other institutions.

It seemed to us that implicit in most microteaching programmes was a model of teaching which contradicted what we took to be the educational values underlying Nuffield Science.

In order to retain those values, we had to devise an alternative programme which allowed for the use of experimental-investigational methods and for teaching which moved from the specific to the general and back again within one unit of activity. Mini-teaching was an attempt to compress the skills that teachers were required to manage in a double-period, Nuffield-style lesson into a fifteen-minute session with a small group of children (about seven).

We brought our study group back to college for a whole day during the second week of the first teaching practice. Our hope was that they had by then got some feeling for the school, and had observed several lessons but had probably not yet had to teach full lessons to whole classes.

We also brought to the centre for the day a class of third or fourth year girls from a comprehensive or secondary modern school, with at least one of their teachers. The students took it in turns to 'teach' a group of six to eight girls for a period of ten to twenty minutes. They chose the topic themselves but we asked them to choose topics which if possible involved some practical activity, and which might lead to some sort of general conclusions within the period of time available.

The 'lessons' were recorded by one fixed television camera, mounted high up in one corner with a sufficiently wide-angle lens to take in the whole scene of action. A diagonal angle allowed us to see the teacher clearly, and the children in at least part profile.

The teacher was recorded from a radio microphone; the setting was a teaching laboratory, not a studio. No one else was in the room except the student and the children. The student not only conducted the class but saw them in, opened and closed the 'lesson', and saw them out. We viewed the lesson in an adjacent room with a television monitor.

The recording was replayed to each student immediately, but we offered to stop it at any point he wished. We made no comments on the lesson before seeing the tape except for social ease — 'How did it go, OK?'. We then took the students' own comments on the tape as our agenda. We approached only very gently areas which struck us as significant but which they did not raise. When interpretations were made from the tapes we sometimes diverged in our own interpretations and left these discrepancies partially unresolved unless the students pursued them.

Generally they were very perceptive, about themselves and about the children. Some students expressed surprise, even distress* at seeing themselves. They were mostly concerned to modify their talk and actions and had the opportunity to repeat the session the same day if they wished to do so. In particular they seemed to notice when their concern for 'appearing to be a teacher' became discordant with the sort of relationship they had with the children.

Tapes were always erased immediately and the students knew this.

Students were asked to record, briefly, their impressions of the day — these were then collated and circulated to the whole group. The comments of the 1971—2 group were as follows:

*See codes of practice.

99

1. *The object was to get across the idea that starch could be broken down in the mouth by saliva, and to see how this was related to digestion as a whole.*

The children enjoyed the experimental work, and appeared to grasp the concepts on the whole. However, as I thought the children would in fact be a year older than they actually were, I had prepared the 'lesson' at a slightly higher level than the children were in fact able to reach. Consequently, there were times when they appeared slightly bewildered as to a point that I was trying to get across.

I felt that the children were far more receptive at the beginning of the lesson, and seemed to grasp all concepts with ease and enthusiasm. However towards the end, although they took a lively interest in the practical work throughout, they seemed to lose the thread of the theoretical material, possibly as I mentioned earlier because the level was just a little too high, or because it in fact took longer to put over the point than I had anticipated. Seeing the tape played back confirmed my suspicions regarding this point, and even more so the fact that when it came to summing up the children were not completely aware that the lesson had come to an end. This last point was probably a reaction to the fact that the experiment had not worked at first, and it was not until after careful observation that the results showed themselves. This created tensions, which manifested themselves in the tone of my voice and probably in my ability to lead the children to their logical conclusions. Generally speaking, the value of the tape was that one sees oneself to some extent objectively (if this is at all possible) so that small phrases that one tends to repeat manifest themselves, and one's own mannerisms are thrust upon oneself. However, probably due to the shock of seeing oneself on tape, I felt that I was far more aware of my mistakes, and far too embarrassed at having myself presented to me to notice any of the good points about my teaching, so that if they had not been pointed out to me, they would have gone by unnoticed.

Another aspect of seeing the videotape was that one sees the pupils from, as it were, another angle. Obviously when one is in the process of teaching, one can only observe the children to a limited extent, but the tape was able to show me far more precisely their reactions to the lessons and who was not paying attention at what point in the proceedings. In this respect such an exercise can be quite a fair guide to the teacher as to how well a lesson is going down with his pupils.

I did not reteach the lesson, due to lack of time, but I felt that I would not have approached the topic differently, but would have merely tried to cut down the length of the less important parts of the lesson, and would have helped the children to their conclusions in a clearer and more concise manner, so that the lesson objectives would come more easily to them.

NB. In retrospect although I felt the tape interesting and useful at the time, I have probably gained just as much if not more from the real classroom situation where the member of staff who is observing you is able to give you constructive criticism, and it is then possible to use the suggestions and criticisms to improve on future lessons.

2. *The surface purpose of my microteach was to get eight 12—13 year old girls from Fulham to discover inductively Euler's theorem for polyhedra, namely v + f = e + 2. (v = No. of vertices, f = No. of faces, e = No. of edges.)*

The idea was that after the preliminary definitions of vertex (corner point), face and edge, they would count the number of each on a selection of assorted polyhedra — cube, tetrahedron, prism, various pyramids. Meanwhile I would be writing up their results on the board. So far so good — now for the tricky bit. When they had finished they were supposed to look at the mass of figures on the blackboard for a minute or two — then have an intuitive flash and deduce the relationship. No such luck. They weren't happy about the idea of an equation, let alone an equation with letters in it. At this point, being short of time, I glossed over the idea of an equation; with the result that I had to all but deduce the relationship myself until one of them saw what I was getting at. It was a bit sad, seeing that they were supposed to be discovering it inductively — so on the surface level it was a failure.

The underlying purpose was for me to get a look at myself (and for you to get some research material?). My atrocious cockney accent came as no surprise to me; the main thing was I was able to observe them observing me. When I was actually teaching I couldn't work on the two levels of teaching and seeing the situation objectively simultaneously. When actually teaching you're more concerned with what you're saying than with how you're saying it. Sad but true.

As a result of the microteach I now try and have part of my brain discorporate itself and observe me, so that I can see myself in their eyes and recognize when I'm going too fast (or too slow) — or mucking it up completely. Kids won't always tell you.

I missed out the last part of the teach-view-discuss-reteach, as I felt that if I were to do it again, it would be with brighter or older children — ones who were happy with the idea of an algebraic equation.

3. Arrive not knowing what to teach, decide on something, ask Clem, am confused as to how much I need to teach. Go away to get equipment and change mind en route, decide on another simpler topic. Girls are third formers, well behaved on the whole. We 'look after' them playing maths games etc. go to animal house and this is really where you get to know them which is a help when teaching. I am to teach third. I go down to prepare, wear microphone behind tie —should the girls know they are on TV or not? They come in, seven of them, three see poster saying 'Are you fat?' and collapse laughing for the rest of the ten-minute lesson. I do a demonstration and try to get across my point which is quite easy as it is very simple. However, I feel it to be too simple and start to involve myself in all sorts of offshoots from the main topic. I start to get confused and scramble back to the the main topic. — 'All I really want to say is . . .' I was told some of my conversation with the girls in the lesson is like Morecambe and Wise. Finish. Watch tape. Amazed at voice and appearance etc. See all the points where I was going wrong and decide to teach in the afternoon — a different set of girls. This time they do the experiment individually and this helps a lot as they are of course immediately involved in something other than 'Are you fat?' posters and disembowelled ladies.* Lesson goes off quite well and this time I try to avoid getting myself sidetracked. This succeeded to a certain extent and again the main point is easily made. I feel more relaxed this second time, and I think an improvement is seen on the screen. Another noticeable point is that when you do feel yourself getting in difficulties you seem to ramble on for a long time getting deeper and deeper but in fact on the screen it doesn't seem half so bad.

I found the whole day very enjoyable in general and useful in certain ways. It was useful because it made you see yourself as others presumably see you. In my case the TV image was not half so bad as the image I had of myself and for about an hour afterwards I felt confident of standing up before children etc. However by the time I came round to teaching at TP school, this confidence had gone, I felt it all to be a sort of pleasant interlude in my TP. My image of myself took over again and I feel in a sense disappointed in

*The laboratory is crowded with equipment and materials — including a life-size plastic 'body' with removable organs.

myself for not being what I saw. Also the 'classroom' was somewhat idealized. Six to seven girls who behaved well, who expected something unusual and even though they didn't get it remained alert to the end of lesson. They didn't bear us any grudge as we were, in a sense, giving them a day off school. Also the voice you employed isn't the one used in a big laboratory containing thirty-five pupils.

Eye contact was discussed after the first viewing — I didn't look at them for about five of the ten minutes. In the second showing I did avoid this fault, but as they were doing the experiment themselves, this was a different situation.

During the playback, I made most of the comments such as 'Oh, my God!' etc. but two tutors made comments which I took note of.

4. Third form girls — they naturally split themselves into groups of five and six.

I took the second group of girls — these were quiet and well behaved — perhaps still in awe of their surroundings. Set out to talk about waves and gave them this as a definite talking point. Introduced the 'slinky'* and let them play with it, showed different kinds of waves — a pulse travelling down and being reflected at the end, also the transverse waves — don't think I actually mentioned the names but emphasized the ways of producing the two kinds — i.e. pushing the slinky and moving it from side to side. Tried to bring out the uses of the waves and wave-like motion — mentioned sound in particular and reminded them of the ball model in the maths laboratory which they had been playing with.

Playback — initial shock of hearing own voice — main thing that came from this was a discussion about an alternative way of presentation.

*Slinky — a child's toy, a long spring made out of a strip of spring steel.

The second time I didn't say what we were going to talk about but just gave them the slinky and a length of tubing to play with. After a few minutes of wild shaking etc., I suggested a way of pushing the slinky and making pulses with the tube and tried to lead the discussion. I asked what we could use waves for and got the immediate answer — 'telephone'.

This group was in fact more lively and realized what was going on. When they just came in they asked 'if they were being filmed and what was that thing round my neck'. Once we started the 'lesson' they were quite happy but they knew when I had finished without my giving any formal conclusion and started to ask me again about the camera and the fish* and anything else.

I enjoyed this session more but to transfer these ideas to school would create certain difficulties. We only had a small group here, multiply that by five then you have to make the choice of who to talk to and when.

I think the girls enjoyed the day and the different surroundings — valuable experience for pupils and students.

5. My choice of what to microteach was not the result of very much thought; I simply wanted to try out something fairly simple with the groups in order to see how easily I could get them going with questions and answers about something they actually had in their hands. In addition this meant that their attention was diverted from me and onto the apparatus in front of them.

In the event the girls made some sense of what they were required to do and even, I think, of the material I was trying to teach, although I felt that their response to the situation was determined more by what they thought was expected of them in this strange situation than by my performance. For my part I did not feel unduly conditioned by the presence of

*There is a fish tank in the room.

the TV camera over and above the general insecurity of relating to a group with which I was unfamiliar.

On the playback I had no difficulty in recognizing myself and no great trauma either. In fact I felt that from the outside the lesson looked more satisfactory, more streamlined, than it felt from the inside. This means, I think, that the technique (the position of the camera, or whatever) was not sufficiently sensitive to the fine detail — the texture — of what was happening, although in conjunction with my own recall of the situation it provided a powerful means of charting on a larger scale the progress of the lesson.

6. I was going to attempt to put over the concept of food chains. For nearly a week I had thought about it, rewritten my notes numerous times and dreamt untold horrors of that dreaded day.

I was selected to be the first of the day, and nervously awaited the girls' arrival. As they came through the door, heart pounding I told them to sit down. Very, very briefly I tried to explain why they were here, but told them nothing about the camera in the corner of the room, nor remarked about the microphone around my neck. My first introductory words to the topic were, of course, 'What are food chains?' I was very surprised to find that they had no idea what they were, and at this point I abandoned the carefully thought up notes, and went my own way. After attempting to explain what food chains were, I did a worked example on the board, and again asked them to define food chains. Although this time they had some idea, it was obvious that they didn't thoroughly understand, this time I asked them to think of food that we eat, and to trace this food back to the plant. When a particular food was chosen on the board, this was repeated a few times. After this I digressed somewhat to food . . . and then asked them what they thought would happen if one population of animals was removed from the food chain; I also asked what population

did they think would flourish. This didn't go down very well, and I had to go right back to the beginning again to explain the concept. Finally I summarized, asking them questions on what we had done.

On seeing myself on the tape I was surprised that I had looked so composed and more in command of the situation than I had supposed. I tended to comment quite a lot on things that I had done, particularly my use of words. For example, it was obvious when played back that flourish was not a suitable word for that occasion. It was suggested that I did it again, using visual aids, but on thinking about it, I didn't feel inspired enough about food chains to do another lesson in a few hours' time.

Although the experience did give me an insight into what I look like teaching, how I project my voice etc., I found that I soon forgot when trying to cope with thirty third year children who were just running riot, and probably seeing myself on a videotape at this particular time would not have been a particularly pleasurable experience.

The mini-teaching exercise was not intended as a total training scheme — it was for us a way of initiating the study group — of establishing a commitment to immediate problems of teaching. Our intention was also to use it as a remedial technique later in the course (which was the way we had first used it a year earlier), but in fact the need for this did not arise.

We were very anxious to protect individual students — in fact when other people at the Centre became interested in developing microteaching we suggested quite a strong code of practice based on our own experience. This code of practice was deliberately rather stringent — the idea was that in experimenting in a new area, where students were particularly vulnerable, it was necessary to have strict guidelines; anyone wishing to depart from the rules would then have to justify their actions explicitly.

Code of practice

1. Microteaching should not be a required part of the course. Students should be free to opt for it if they wish, and to request it when they feel they need it, but they should not be expected, or coerced, into taking part.

2. There should be no formal assessment of microteaching performance.

3. Initial viewing of the tapes should be by the student and whoever is responsible for supervising him/her during microteaching. No one else should be present.

4. Copyright of all recordings should be with the student. As a general practice tapes should be erased. If they are retained they should never be replayed without the student's full permission.

5. No one should be in the room during the recording except the student and the children.

An exploration in the use of videotape recording in teacher-pupil relationships (by Robert Jardine, from *Visual Education* March 1972, p. 21)

We worked with three groups of pupils, aged twelve to thirteen and fourteen to fifteen, and three teachers. We asked that each session should last for at least two periods, and as we did not wish to disrupt lessons more than necessary, groups were chosen who normally had a double period of English at some time during the week which could be devoted to the project. (There was no drama course as such, drama lessons forming part of the English syllabus.)

Over a period of about a term and a half we carried out five sessions with one group, seven with the second group, and ten with the third group. At the beginning of the project we made several visits to each group, observing the pupils and teachers in action, before we began video recording. During this period we discussed procedural details with the three teachers. We wanted the project to be an extension of their drama work, rather than an isolated experiment, since we felt that the latter course offered less scope for integration into the overall syllabus. The procedure which we adopted was to record the pupils improvising a dramatic situation. A Sony portable camera and battery-operated half-inch videotape recorder were used, with a mains vtr and monitor for playbacks. Usually, we operated the camera with a pupil holding the extension microphone. The cameraman was guided by a 'director' who was either the teacher or one of the pupils. The videotape was replayed during the second half of the lesson, followed by a discussion which was also recorded. If the pupils wanted to develop the play at the next session we would begin by replaying the previous week's discussion. Alternatively, they would spend some time during the week preparing new themes for the next session. The typical sequence which emerged was: improvise and record play — playback — discuss and record. The procedure was, however, kept flexible. Sometimes we would stop halfway through an improvisation in order to play back what had happened so far. Occasionally we began a session by showing a tape made with one of the other groups.

From our observations in class and from talking with the teachers we learned that they usually approached their drama lessons in one of two ways. One way was to give the pupils an initial situation or theme and let them improvise a play around it, choosing roles and deciding on the development of the plot. Another way was to tell them a complete story which they then acted out, making modifications if they so wished. As we wanted to encourage a dialectical relationship between pupils and teachers (while not causing a disruption of the ongoing situation) one of the strategies which we suggested, based on the above procedures, was as follows:

1. The teacher prepares the lesson as a complete story with a beginning A, a middle B, and an end C.

2. At the start of the lesson the pupils are given part A only. They then develop the play themselves and act it out, and a videotape recording is made of the play with its new middle B1 and ending C1.

3. The tape is played back immediately and the two stories ABC and AB1C1 form the basis of a discussion between teacher and pupils.

At a session with her group, Joyce, one of the teachers, decided to try this approach. She had worked out a story and written a brief scenario for the play. As she had not done any prior preparation with the group she outlined each scene before they began. During the course of the play she occasionally butted in if she thought the action was straying from the point, or if she was not happy with their characterizations. In the latter case she merely asked them whether they really felt they were playing true to character rather than telling them they were wrong. Although they were not encouraged to stray from the point of the situation they were allowed to digress from the teacher's version of the story (of which they were only sketchily aware) and to introduce any developments which they saw fit. When Joyce judged that each scene had run its course she interjected the beginning of the next scene. Her scenario and the play as acted out by the pupils are compared in Figure 1.

There is a significant difference in 'John's' age and social position in the two versions. In the teacher's version

FIGURE 1

Teacher's version	Pupils' version
Scene i. John, a schoolboy, is persuaded by two friends to help them commit a burglary.	John, who has already spent five years in prison, is persuaded by two friends to help them commit a burglary.
Scene ii. The owner of the house surprises them. He does not try to catch them as he recognizes John.	The owner surprises them, grabs John, scuffles with him and overpowers him.
Scene iii. John is being questioned at the police station. His teacher refuses to stand bail on the grounds that he cannot trust John not to run away.	John is being questioned at the police station. He tells the police he is an engineer. He phones his former teacher and she agrees to stand bail.
Scene iv. John's mother and father	At this point the two 'friends' suggest that the police should bring them in for questioning. The group agrees. The police arrive at a club frequented by the friends. Lesson ends.
Scene v. Back at school the teacher who refused to help tries to be friendly but John is curt with him.	
Scene vi. John's school friends.	

he is still a schoolboy; in the pupils' version he is an engineer with a previous conviction. In Joyce's story there is a pointed lack of violence; the opposite is true of the pupils' version. Also, there are significant differences in the role and sex of the 'teacher' in the two versions.

We knew from speaking with the teachers that the themes which they chose often reflected their own current real-life preoccupations (this case was a striking example) and we supposed that the same would be true for the pupils. Later experience confirmed this. A comparison of the teacher's version of the play and the pupils' version allows each to gain insight into the experiential world of the other. This encourages dialogue between pupil and teacher in place of instruction of the pupils by the teacher. In the latter case there is always the danger that there may be too great a disparity between the teacher's world and that of the pupils with the result that the teacher is in a position of forcing his view of the world on to the pupils and communication breaks down.

Alternatively, the teacher may choose themes which he thinks reflect the pupils' imaginings and real life preoccupations. These, too, may be unrelated to the pupils' ideas. Both these possibilities indicate a lack of understanding of the pupils by the teacher which can only be avoided when they have a dialectical relationship to each other.

As the project progressed, other techniques of encouraging dialogue between pupils and teachers began to suggest themselves. From the start we had recorded the discussion which followed the playback of the videotape of the improvisation. At most sessions we replayed this second tape as well. During the recording of the play, the cameraman was usually under the direction of a teacher or one of the pupils who indicated when he should stop recording at the end of scenes or sequences of action.

Later on in the project, however, we continued recording after the director had shouted 'Cut!', so that the finished videotape contained, along with other 'extraneous' activity, all the interruptions made by the teacher during the course of the play. Thus we had a record of teacher-pupil interaction at all stages of the session. The 'performance' to be discussed following the replay was not, therefore, the pupils' improvisation but the drama lesson itself.

Not surprisingly, it proved rather difficult to get the pupils to discuss the teachers' performances' recorded on videotape as interruptions in their plays. I do not think that this was because they were reticent or afraid but rather because it seldom occurred to them to do so. Most of the pupils' comments were directed at themselves or at each other. Some of these give an indication of the initial impact of self-viewing: 'When I was on the videotape I thought I was smaller than what I already am.' 'Seeing myself on "tele" is quite good but some people may think it's not you. On videotape you look a lot different and you sound it.' Other comments suggest that self-communication, or feedback, by means of instant video replay, can have an educative effect: 'When I saw myself on tape it was exciting to watch myself do things wrong, instead of people telling me I'm wrong.' After watching a tape of her group, a girl commented that she had talked too much. By dominating the play in this way she had prevented the others from developing their roles. The following week, although she played the same kind of role she cut her share of the talking down by more than half.

During in-class discussions, the teachers' remarks were also usually aimed at the pupils' improvisations. Sometimes, though, they would talk about their own 'performances' but this was usually to us, not in front of the pupils. For example, Mary pointed out her tendency to talk all the time in class as a kind of defence just to keep the pupils quiet. Joyce felt that she 'interrupted too much' and made 'value judgements' about the improvisation rather than practical suggestions. On one occasion, during a discussion in class, she expressed an opinion which was not immediately taken up by the group. A few minutes later she mentioned it again but attributed the opinion to one of the girls. She had not been aware of this at the time and would not have realized it but for the video recording.

Walter, the third teacher, felt that he was not getting on so well with his pupils as Joyce appeared to. He did not know whether this was because of them, or whether it had something to do with him. He suspected that it was his fault. He sometimes got the impression that he was 'going over their heads'.

The feedback process which occurs during self-viewing on a video monitor has been utilized in recent years in microteaching techniques. In conventional microteaching, however, the trainee teacher usually discusses his recorded performance with a supervisor and/or other trainee teachers. While this may make the teacher more aware of himself and enable him to improve his performance as an instructor it does not give him anything like a full understanding of his relationship with the pupils in his class. Instructional teaching alone is not sufficient to communicate both cognitive and emotive understanding because such understanding develops out of a two-way process.

Education is a function of the teacher-pupil relationship. If education is to contribute significantly to the realization of cognitive and emotive potential in pupils and teachers, that is to say, if it is to be creative, then the conditions must exist for dialogue between teachers and pupils. Video playback in conventional microteaching gives the teacher a new perspective on his own actions and the behaviour of the pupils in his class. It does not allow these perspectives to be checked dialectically against the pupils' perspectives of their own and the teacher's actions. What we were attempting to do was to increase the possibility of dialogue and its effectiveness by bringing video feedback into the classroom. Within the relatively brief period of the project we were only partially successful in this.

Our experience of ourselves consists only partly of our experience of our own feelings, thoughts, intentions, desires and actions. In our relationships with others there is, in addition to this direct self-experience, an indirect component which is our view of the other person's view of us, mediated through his behaviour. Our self-identity, which is what we feel we are, and what we feel ourselves to be for others, is a synthesis of these direct and indirect components.

However, self-identity is not based on the totality of our own perceptions, feelings, thoughts, intentions, desires and actions, nor on the totality of other people's behaviour towards us. Experience is selective. Consciously or unconsciously, we include certain aspects of the interpersonal situation in our experience of self and other, while excluding other aspects. We may also exaggerate or play down those aspects which we include. Depending on which aspects we include and which aspects we exclude from our experience of self, the self which we feel ourselves to be, and which we feel ourselves to be for others, may or may not coincide with the way others really see us.

Videotape enables us to make recordings of sequences of personal interaction which include the totality of each person's verbal, gestural and postural communication to the other(s). It conveys the nuances of meaning in vocal inflexions, facial expressions and the movements of the eyes, hands and body. Videotape also enables us to play back this record instantly, rather like the 'action replays' which have become commonplace in television coverage of sporting events. The technique is one with which we are all familiar: certain parts of the race, game or whatever, are replayed immediately after they happen, sometimes in slow motion, so that viewers can build up a clearer picture of what happened. The viewer may even change his mind about what he has just seen as a result of the replay.

The replay may be repeated several times, both during and after the event. For example, during the television 'post mortem' on a football match, parts of the event are again selected for playback. At the same time, the players involved may be invited into the studio to 'talk us through' what we are watching on the screen. In this way not only we, the spectators, but also the players themselves get a new perspective on what happened.

With videotape, we can make recordings of interpersonal communication, replay them, and invite each person involved to talk us through what he sees himself doing and what he sees the others doing. His new perspective on his own and the others' actions is based on a complete behavioural record which is a common reference for each person. Each person's experience will still, of necessity, be selective, but the selection is open to checking and modification in the light of subsequent replays and of the perspectives of others. On television you look and sound different than you think you look and sound. Laughter, surprise, embarrassment, disappointment, are among the most common reactions to self-viewing. They are the concomitants of a change of viewpoint or 'mind' on one's own behaviour and the behaviour of others. During the replay, each person can draw the other's attention towards details of communicative behaviour and the interpretations derived from them which they may have omitted from their perspectives.

Bob Jardine's account expresses well the direction our ideas were moving on the basis of our experience of mini-teaching.

The mini-teaching exercise and pre- and post-teaching practice discussions created ideas to pursue for the rest of the term. One immediate development was the 'communication games'.

COMMUNICATION GAMES

We developed communication games to experience and practise particular social skills apparently involved in classroom communication. The skills themselves were isolated from discussions of teaching practice, from the mini-teaching exercise, or from viewing films and tapes of lessons. We tried to construct games that demanded sensitivity to changes in social context and monitoring of the actions of self and others.

Most of these games are not strictly role-play or simulation games — they tend not to demand skilful dramatic performances or working through complex materials. They are intended to idealize and amplify critical facets of communication; not to foster 'acting' or the temporary suspension of reality.

In role-play games the aim is to act in ways that create and sustain situations and identities outside the immediate context. In these games the emphasis is less on the creation of identities than on the participant's actual identity for self and others, and on specific means by which participants communicate — the emphasis is on the situation rather than the role of the person. In G. H. Mead's terms they involve 'role taking' rather than 'role playing'.

The games are often indeterminate — repeated playing leads to alternative outcomes. One attempt at playing them will rarely exhaust their potential; what it will raise will be particular issues and problems which can be explored through repeated playing of the same game or through other games. This means that students and tutors should be prepared to devise their own games.

We have presented the games in an order that reflects the subtlety of their content and difficulty of their realization. We are not necessarily advocating that they should be played in this order (or even played at all). The order is one we have constructed in retrospect, not necessarily the order we devised and used them in.

For a group unused to the games it is useful to have some 'warm-up games' with which to open the session. We have used two games devised by Ed Berman's 'Interaction' organisation — 'Lawyer' and 'Policeman'; both have relevance for teaching.

1. Lawyer

Anyone who has been in court will recognize the relevance of the title — witnesses are required to answer one person while looking at another. The group sits in a close circle, one person stands in the centre firing questions and keeping close eye contact with whoever he is asking (A). Whoever is sitting immediately to the right of (A) has to answer the question as though they were (A). By rapidly switching the person being asked, the 'lawyer' can create a complicated communication pattern. Everyone taking part has to concentrate hard on the direction of eye contact and its relation to talk.

(We first used the game after observing a teacher looking at one child — as a control device — while talking to others.)

There are a number of ways of extending 'Lawyer'. The group can divide into pairs and try conversing side by side and back to back. The pairs can separate into two groups,

one of the pair on each side of the room, and try conversing as loud and/or as softly as possible. All these games focus attention on talk itself as a somewhat problematic means of communication. Another variant — which we first learnt from Keith Johnson's Actors' Workshop at the Royal Court Theatre — we call 'Keep talking'. Students, in pairs, take it in turns to keep the other talking. Used well this can bring into awareness areas of thought often not realized.

2. Policeman

Policeman is a 'group memory' game. The policeman stands in the middle of the circle extracting details of the crime from different people (name, age, address, occupation, where were you at 8.00 p.m.?). Soon he begins to repeat questions, but asking different members, so that everyone, including the 'policeman', has to remember what everyone else says.

3. Who's talking?

This game was devised by the study group because some students said they had found it difficult in formal situations to tell exactly who was talking in class.

The group sits in pairs in two rows all facing forwards. The 'teacher' goes out of the room for a few minutes while the group decides who is talking to whom. The teacher enters the room, sits at the front of the rows, about 6 feet back from the front, and has the problem of locating talk partners. The rule is that she can move people from seat to seat and once talk partners are seated side by side they have to stop talking. The game ends when all talk partners are sitting side by side and there is 'quiet'.

4. A role-play game

We have devised several games which attempt to create role playing situations using cues written on cards. The cards attempt to define a 'grammar' within which transaction can take place. The instructions are 'rules' that generate situations but allow the development of incidents some indeterminacy.

1. **You are a pupil**
   Try to change the content and/or direction of the lesson. You can only talk when the teacher asks you to.

2. **You are a pupil**
   Every third question the teacher asks — put your hand up.

3. **You are a pupil**
   Try to change the content and/or direction of the lesson. You can only talk when the teacher asks you to.

4. **You are a pupil**
   Every second question the teacher asks — put your hand up.
   If the teacher has a characteristic gesture — ask him/her why he/she does it.

5. **You are a pupil**
   You feel sympathy for the teacher in the face of pupils who are trying to disrupt the lesson. Find ways of encouraging the teacher.

6. **You are the teacher**
   You cannot start the lesson until someone asks you a question nor can you end it until one of the pupils gives you a signal. Everyone else is playing a pupil role.

7. **You are a pupil**
   Try to become the centre of attraction in the class. You must do what the teacher asks you to do.

8. **You are a pupil**
   Every third question the teacher asks — put your hand up.

9. **You are a pupil**
   Every class has 'ringleaders' — kids who are the centre of attraction. Identify the ringleaders in this lesson and try to find ways of attracting their attention and spurring them on.

10. **You are a pupil**
    Every class has 'ringleaders' — kids who are the centre of attraction. Identify the ringleaders here and try to encourage them.

11. **You are a pupil**
    Your role is to end the lesson.*

12. **You are a pupil**
    Try to get the teacher to talk to you in a one-to-one relationship. Count how many times you succeed — and how many times the teacher uses your name.

13. **You are a pupil**
    The lesson cannot start until you ask the teacher a question.
    Try and keep the lesson following the direction you want to follow.

This game was a response to students' comments about the difficulty of establishing themselves as 'looking like a teacher', especially in the way they entered and initiated lessons. The first play with this set of cards — which forces the teacher into identifying him/herself non-verbally — is usually stalemate. No one knows who the teacher is, and the teacher cannot identify him/herself. This raises as a problem the way in which teachers can walk into a classroom or a corridor filled with children and command attention without actually saying anything. Further plays reveal other issues, especially around the theme of varieties in pupil role and identity. Games 5 and 7 arose in this way.

*This card is ambiguous as it can be taken to mean 'disrupt the lesson totally' or to say something like 'please miss it's time for break'. This kind of ambiguity is one of the things that allows the games to be replayed, continuously modifying the rules.

Gestures can be expressive, puzzling or ambiguous

The games involving perception of gestures and other non-verbal signs may seem, at first sight, to be peripheral to problems of teaching, but close study of films, videotapes or photographs from classrooms reveals the full complexity and significance of non-verbal signs.

111

5. Another role-play game

Someone from the group leaves the room for a few minutes to prepare a 'five-minute lesson'. The rest of the group decide the kinds of pupils in the class (e.g. attentive, helpful, non-attentive, aggressive, bored, clown etc.). Usually the student who suggests the role is willing to play it. The group is rearranged so that, for example, an attentive pupil is sandwiched between two non-attentive ones. The 'teacher' is brought into the room and presented with dual task of trying to teach the lesson and trying to identify the roles each member of the group is playing. The person playing teacher has to continually scan, listen and assess the actions of others — each of his own actions becomes a probe to test the reactions of others — each of his own actions becomes a probe to test the reactions that result from it. The success with which students, and more experienced teachers, play pupil parts always surprises us.

6. A context awareness game

One or two members of the group leave the room while the rest decide on a social context and their roles within it (a 'doctor's waiting room, bus queue, railway carriage, social security office etc.). The scene is set in such a way that the main communication mode is talk, with little indication given as to who is talking to whom, or their relationship. The outsiders are brought in, have to identify the situation by listening to the talk and then join in, eventually initiating appropriate changes in topic.

7.

A member of the group leaves the room to prepare a 'five-minute lesson'. The rest of the group assign themselves pupil roles. A critical change is made that makes the 'lesson' impossible (chalk and blackboard duster removed, a pupil is continually referred to who is absent etc.). The teacher has to notice the 'unusual' aspect of the classroom and devise strategies which induce the pupils to rectify his problem. For example, if the chalk is missing the teacher has to identify the 'culprit'; or in the other case to realize that the person constantly being referred to is absent. (A rule may be introduced which allows everyone to lie but the real culprit.)

8.

This game was devised to meet the need for practice in perception of non-verbal actions. The game requires participants to scan continuously in order tp perceive the cues which form the sequence. At some points in the game there are choices which must be made appropriate to that particular performance of the game. Everyone is given a card which marks a series (here six) of paired cues and actions: Those holding cards with many spaces are given at least one marker cue (e.g. card 5 has 'yawn'). The marker cue serves to confirm the participants' perceptions of the progress of the sequence.

The game needs a suitable seating plan, which depends on the number involved (we find fourteen the maximum). Usually the first point raised by this game is how to clear communication channels — the sequence may be masked by participants' 'normal' non-verbal actions.

There are two sorts of cue:

A cue that participant has to perform before others can respond.

A marker cue.

1.

	Cues which participant emits	Actions (participants' responses — select one)
a	Rub chin	
b	Lean back in chair	Move chair back Move chair to side Turn chairs
c		
d		
e	Twiddle thumbs	Clap hands Pick fingers Point
f		

2.

a	[Rub chin]	
b	Lean back in chair	Rub nose / Rub eyes / Rub cheeks
c		
d	[Yawn]	
e		Cough / Click / Blow
f		

3.

a		
b	[Lean back on chair]	Move chair back / Move chairs to side / Turn chairs
c	Cross feet	
d		
e	[Twiddle thumbs]	Clap hands / Pick fingers / Point
f		

4.

a		
b		Stamp foot / Rub feet on floor / Take off shoe
c	[Cross feet]	
d		
e	Twiddle thumbs	
f		

5.

a		
b		
c		
d	Yawn	
e		
f	[Close eyes briefly]	Look up / Look round / Look down

7.

a		
b	Lean back on chair	Move chair back / Move chair to side / Turn chairs
c		
d	Yawn	Cough / Click / Blow
e		
f		

9.

a		
b		
c	Cross feet	Stamp foot / Rub feet on floor / Take off shoe
d		
e	Twiddle thumbs	Clap hands / Pick fingers / Point
f		

6.

a		
b		
c		
d	Yawn	Cough / Click / Blow
e	Twiddle thumbs	Clap hands / Pick fingers / Point
f	Close eyes	

8.

a	Rub chin	Rub nose / Rub eyes / Rub cheeks
b		
c		
d		
e		
f		

10.

a	
b	
c	
d	Yawn
	Cough Click Blow
e	
f	

11.

a	
b	
c	
d	Twiddle thumbs
	Clap hands Pick fingers Point
e	
f	

12.

	Cues	Actions
a		
b		
c		
d		
e		
f	Close eyes briefly	Look up Look round Look down

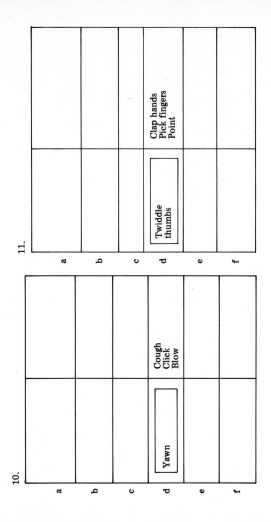

9.

This game is a refined version of game 8 devised by some of the students in one study group.

A group of about ten sit spaced out round a table. The spaces are marked 1 to 10. A set of cards numbered 1 to 10 are shuffled and given out. One card is marked 'start'. Thus the person in seating position 3 might get card 6, and the person in position 10 might get card 4 (start). The person with the start card begins a pre-decided discussion/argument. The next person to talk (in this case) will be the one with card 10, i.e. the same card number as the seating position of the speaker. All participants are induced to talk in a way that sustains the discussion.

This group also succeeded in playing a highly complex game based on game 8. A set of actions was listed and charted as alternatives on a diagram. Cards were then made out with cues and responses, each of the fifteen cues usually having two alternative responses. The eight resulting cards enabled participants to create a cyclic game with no rigid sequencing as in game 8.

Actions

1. Yawn
2. Cross feet
3. Lean back in chair
4. Sigh
5. Rub eyes
6. Look at watch
7. Lean chin on hands
8. Twiddle thumbs
9. Bite nails
10. Put hands behind head
11. Cough
12. Scratch back
13. Scratch foot
14. Push fingers through hair
15. Move chair

Pathways

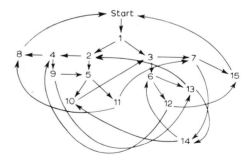

1 → 2/3	2 → 4/5	3 → 6/7	4 → 8/9
5 → 10/11	6 → 12/13	7 → 14/15	8 → 1
9 → 13/5	10 → 3	11 → 7/8	12 → 4/15
13 → 14/2	14 → 10/6	15 → 1	

1.

Yawn	Cross feet *or* lean back in chair
Cough	Lean chin on hands *or* twiddle thumbs

2.

Cross feet	Sigh *or* rub eyes
Scratch back	Sigh *or* move chair

3.

Put hands behind head	Lean back on chair
Look at watch	Scratch back *or* scratch foot

4.

	Start yawn
Sigh	Twiddle thumbs
Bite nails	Scratch foot *or* rub eyes

5.

Rub eyes	Put hands behind head *or* cough
Scratch foot	Cross feet

6.

Move chair	Yawn
Push fingers through hair	Put hands behind head *or* look at watch

7.

Lean chin on hands	Push fingers through hair *or* move chair
Sigh	Bite nails

8.

Lean back on chair	Look at watch *or* lean chin on hands
Twiddle thumbs	Yawn

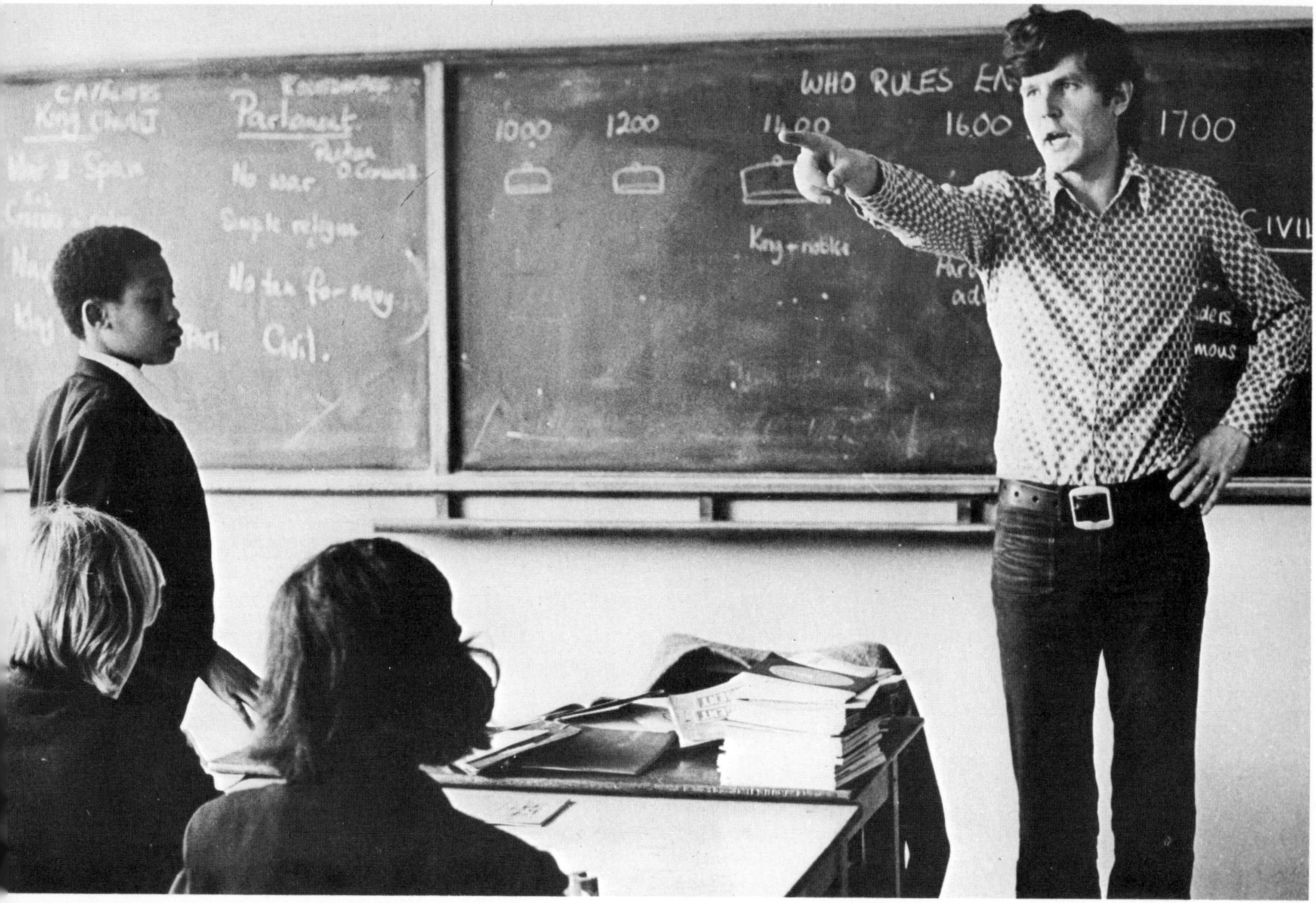
WHO RULES
1000
1200
1600
1700
Parliament
Civil.

Varieties of the sign 'teacher points'

Various signs involving 'hand to face'

A DESCRIPTION OF A LEARNING GAME
From chapter 17 of *The University Crisis Reader*, Vol. 1, edited by Immanuel Wallerstein and Paul Starr (Random House, 1971).

Radical critics have challenged not just the content of liberal education, but its form as well, maintaining that authoritarian learning patterns emasculate students, blunt their energies and imagination, and prepare them for authoritarian patterns of government and social behaviour. The critics have argued that all too often schooling produces no genuine education but rather one long exercise in pleasing teachers and carrying out instructions. In *The Student as Nigger*, a classic indictment of formal education, Jerry Farber made precisely this point: '[Students] haven't gone through twelve years of public school for nothing. They've learned one thing and perhaps only one thing during those twelve years. They've forgotten their algebra. They're hopelessly vague about chemistry and physics. They've grown to fear and resent literature. They write like they've been lobotomized. But, Jesus, can they follow orders!'

Michael Rossman, a leader of the Free Speech Movement at Berkeley in 1964, has been another fierce exponent for radical change in classroom authority relations. In an interview in *Change* magazine in 1969, Rossman answered a charge by Morris Abram, President of Brandeis, that he was copping out by ignoring the electoral system with these words: 'You give me control of what happens in the classroom, baby, you let me write and speak and touch people in such a fashion that it changes classroom relations and basic authority relations, and I'll give you the entire electoral system. You aren't going to have a chance: I'm going to have your kids. And I'm going to make your kids able to talk to each other in such a way that they're capable

for the first time of coping with democracy on a mass scale. You're just messing around with the surface of social change.'

One of the techniques that Rossman and others have used in trying to overcome existing patterns of classroom interaction is described in the first article reprinted below. The technique is a 'learning game' in which students and an organizer act out the roles of 'good student' and 'good teacher'. In the process, they analyse their own actions as characteristic responses of people performing those classroom roles. This self-analysis produces tension and 'role-confusion' as the players become more acutely aware of their own inauthenticity and 'role-conditioning'. Finally, the game breaks down, each engaged participant emotionally shaken. But even then the group finds it has not escaped the classroom authority structure, for whenever 'the organizer tries to contribute his knowledge or feelings, the geometry of control snaps back into existence'. Nevertheless, Rossman sees the game as a valuable 'deconditioning' experience which forces the players 'to realize that their social performance as a "good student" has little to do with whatever *being* a good learner actually means to each individual'.

The effort to democratize the classroom and create a more informal, less structured mode of authority has met strong criticism from many educators, including some sympathetic to radical politics. Robert Brustein, dean of the Yale Drama School and a signer of the 'Call to Resist Illegitimate Authority', decried what he saw as a mistaken application of democratic ideals to the educational process and a trend toward idolization of the amateur as a cultural model. Brustein contended that 'the concept of professionalism is being vitiated by false analogies. Because some authority is cruel, callow or indifferent (notably the government in its treatment of certain urgent issues of the day), the Platonic ideal of authority comes under attack.'

In reply to Brustein, Eric Bentley interpreted his colleague's remarks as a turn toward 'defensive conservatism'. Brustein answered that his feelings on the war and other social issues were unchanged, but that he questioned whether the tendency of radical students 'to concentrate on the purification of the universities' would lead to a resolution of those larger problems.

The totalitarian classroom — a learning game
Among the many learning games which young freelance educators are now introducing on campuses is one called Totalitarian Classroom. It depends on the depth to which students (and teachers) have been blindly conditioned to play the social game 'good teacher/good student' which dominates formal education. T.C. is in fact a deconditioning game against this, and its players experience a painful and illuminating perspective on the roles and processes through which they normally move.

The Totalitarian Classroom begins when its organizer announces to a group of from twelve to twenty innocents:

'I want to lead you in a learning game. Whoever plays Totalitarian Classroom with me must follow a small set of rules and roles, which form a stage. Inside this stage, let's try to hold a real discussion of a specific subject: how people act out their parts in the classroom game called 'good student'. First I want to describe the few rules and roles of our own game, and ask you to agree to them. Then we'll start the discussion itself; maybe we can carry it on to consider what the 'good student' game has to do with good learning, if anything.

'The two rules come from assuming that everyone's a "good student". That means he's independent, critical, he has his own unique viewpoint. So I'm always free to ask any of you to express a view that differs from one just given by someone — you can extend him, contradict him, whatever. And likewise, a "good student" is in command of the material and

can make connections between its parts. So I can call on anyone to explain the connection between any two points other people have previously made.'

Of course, the organizer need have no idea whether such points are in fact connectible: that's not his problem. He doesn't mention this, but goes on to ask for volunteers to play three standard 'good student' roles.

'One way to present yourself as a "good student" is to display your command of the material. Another is to brown-nose, to agree with the teacher. But you can also win points by creative disagreement in the classroom game. So we'll want a Scribe, to take absolutely verbatim notes. And a Yes man. When I ask him, about any statement, "Is that right, Mr Yes?" his job will be to say, "Yes, that is right", and then *explain why*. Likewise we'll want a No man, whose job will be to say, when asked, "No, that is wrong", and then explain why. Is all that clear?.

'Are the rest of us supposed to play roles?' someone asks.

'No. No one else should try to play-act a role. Everyone is free to respond as who they are — even the three people who'll volunteer to play these formal roles that are the game's stage, even they should respond as themselves except when I call on them specifically in role. As ourselves, let's try to keep the discussion as real and substantive as we can. I'll try to use the two rules in this way too.'

He calls on these few roles and rules at will, to punctuate or speed up the game, as well as to advance the discussion: they are the formal trace of his control (which extends far beyond them in fact) and they create a stage for theatre. With practice, simply establishing their power is sufficient, and the game may be brought to its desired effect while calling on them rarely.

Typically the volunteers for Yes and No man depend on these strategies naturally. As discussion develops, other players will also assume them unconsciously. The organizer exposes this, after first using them to guide the discussion as he pleases. Often no one will volunteer as Scribe. Insisting that verbatim transcription is essential — which is almost true, since the richest examples of 'good student' performance lie in the precise words people choose for their responses — the organizer drives the group into a democratic election to burden someone with the job. Later he pokes the Scribe with questions, illustrating how impossible it is to think or respond during the process of recording material for playback.

When the discussion begins, the organizer is in total control, no matter how gently or jovially he may have introduced T.C. He is marked as the Expert, bankrolled with specialized Knowledge, the Man Who Knows What Should Happen. He does nothing to inflate or dispel the illusion, but leads the game through its three phases. In the first, by asking questions and giving hints, he gets people to describe in detail the ways in which 'good students' act out their roles in the classroom theatre.

'Very well. What are some ways that people project themselves as "good students" in the classroom?'

'They come to class on time.' 'They hand in their homework.'

'Yes, yes. Some others.'

'Eye contact with the teacher is very important — so is volunteering information.' 'Coming up to him after class to talk about something.'

'What about the way people look? You — how do you look when you've just been asked a question you can't answer but you don't want the teacher to know you haven't thought about it.'

'I sit up straight and wrinkle my forehead, searching — maybe he'll speak first.'

'And you?'

'I lean forward a little and look earnest, and try to talk about something else . . .'

'And you?'

Soon the discussion reveals that different choices of where to sit, of posture, dress and expression, of complaisant or sarcastic attitude, and so on, are rich elements in a variety of styles of projecting oneself to a teacher and class as a 'good student.' The organizer leads the group on, to recognize reinforcing elements and to complete strategies.

'What might go with sitting in the back row and looking out the window, to project a whole "good student" image?'

'Missing a lot of classes but seeing the professor in his offices, maybe not during regular hours.'

'You, I don't know your name, can you give me an independent opinion? No? Well, you next to her, can you?'

'Being casual with your homework, but sparkling on the final.'

'You — what's the connection between the last two answers? Explain.'

'Both times you're showing that you know what's important.'

'Very good! This strategy will work with every teacher, is that right, Mr No?'

'No, that is wrong, it'll only work with some.'

'Because?'

'Because some teachers are uptight about petty detail.'

'In other words, what's important is what *they* think's important. I take it you use this strategy yourself?'

'Something like that.'

'All right. So it's clear different strategies work with different teachers, and different classes too — they're part of the audience too. Now who can say why? What determines whether a projection of yourself as "good student" will be successful, besides skill?'

'If it helps the teacher play his own role well, if it complements his role.'

'Is that right, Mr Yes?'

'Yes, that is right, because then it satisfies his image of himself, it feeds his ego.'

'Is that your real opinion, or your role speaking?'

'Yes' (after some hesitation).

'Then does the image or role of a "good student" necessarily resemble the image of the "good teacher" he's facing?'

'No.'

'Can you give an example? . . . Can anyone?'

'What about the freak in class, and the scholarly professor who translates the freak's occasional insights — which of course *he* recognizes — so the rest of the dull class can understand them?'

'That'll do.'

Soon the group is fully caught up in the roles and rhythms of an academic seminar. From here T.C. passes easily into its second phase of *reflexive theatre*, of play which comments upon its own performance.

'How long do you think it takes to figure out what a teacher expects from you, what "good student" roles you can play with him? Someone: how long?'

'Maybe like three weeks.'

'Anyone think the time is shorter? You do, huh. How short?'

'Oh, you can tell where most teachers are at within the first day or so.'

'Tell him why you think it isn't three weeks.'

'The way he talks about midterms and homework. How he's dressed, whether he wants to bullshit a bit or get right down to the subject. Things like that.'

'Why did you say that looking at me, when I asked you to explain it to him?'

'Because . . . I don't know.'

'Did that explanation make sense to you, do you see why three weeks is too long an estimate?'

'Yes. I can see that it starts right at the beginning. Like whether the teacher asks the class questions about themselves.'

'Wait . . . what is there about what he just said, that is a presentation of himself as "good student"?'

'He admits his mistake.'

'Anyone have a better answer?'

'He not only admits it, he shows he's learned by adding something new.'

'Right on! Now go back. When I asked five of you how you looked when trying not to show you didn't know the answer to a question, everyone gave a different answer — showing they were individual, that's very good. But everyone answered in words. No one demonstrated the look itelf, even though you know how many words a picture's worth. How come you didn't?'

'You wanted us to answer in words.'

'How do you know? As a matter of fact, I was hoping someone wouldn't. Someone else.'

'I think it's because you're articulate.'

'How is that a "good student" response?'

'He was uncertain and afraid you'd tell him he was wrong, so he took care to qualify it.'

'Right. But I think he's right. Can you go on? I mean, how does my being articulate work?'

'What do you mean?'

'I mean . . . No, let's get at this a different way.' (The organizer changes ground whenever he wants; he is in control and need never appear at a loss for words.) 'The other side of the "good student" game is the "good teacher" game. So: in what ways have I been presenting myself as a "good teacher" here?'

'You seem to know what you're doing.' 'You care what people say, and try to draw them out.'

'Thanks for feeding my ego. Something more impersonal?'

'Well, first, you stand at the front and you're always moving, that way we have to focus on you. Secondly, you look people in the eye — that's how you call on them to speak, too. Third, you keep trying to probe deeper for answers. Fourth, . . .'

'Stop right there. Can someone tell me: how is he projecting himself as a "good student", what elements is he projecting?'

'I'm not playing "good student".'

'I don't think you're trying to. But I'm not asking you. Someone else?'

'He volunteered.' 'He's observant and original.'

'Something less trivial.'

'He said "first, second, third . . .".'

'Right on! How is that a presentation of himself as a "good student?"'

'It shows he has an orderly mind.'

'Do you *always* say "first, second, third . . ."?'

'No.'

'Why did you say it here? How did I cue that response?'

'You speak like that, even though you don't say the numbers.'

'Hmmm . . . in what way was that a presentation-of-self-as-good-student?'

'He gave you a sharp answer, even though it might have displeased you personally.'

'How do you know that strategy's a good one to choose with me?'

'Because of how long your hair is.'

'Yes, I pride myself on my tolerance. But I talk like a pedant still, so he knows to give a pedantic answer, right?'

The players, and the organizer himself, have been deeply conditioned. They cannot discuss the game without at the same time playing it. While trying to keep the discussion unfolding with substance and logic, the organizer calls constant attention to the way people act out the only roles they know how to assume in a context of directed and goal-oriented learning. Pressure and pain mount in this second phase, sometimes amazingly. The players become confused and frustrated, as they struggle to keep going with responses whose conditioned nature someone may at any time eagerly and accurately point out. Asked, 'Is that you speaking now, or a role?' they often complain in anguish that they do not know.

The group gives them no help. Initially curious and open, its members are withdrawn with anger and closed. Sharp questions have goosed them impatiently through the organizer's programmed knowledge, making them feel slightly stupid. Fellow members have vied to tear their answers down or give better ones. Reward now means simply to be left alone; punishment, to be called upon by the finger of Authority to answer, isolated and uncertain. Only the Teacher's Pet is at ease. (I have seen no one, however skilled, manage to avoid generating a Pet relationship with at least one player while directing T.C. The conditioning runs deep.)

The organizer's absolute control is only reaffirmed when he points out gently the scornful violence he has been doing to individuals, their willingness to accept it, and the usual fact that no one has faced or addressed another player directly, or defended or supported another against attack. People try to break past their role confusion, but cannot: the organizer skillfully co-opts any argument or objection to further the game itself, using the 'let's talk about it, why are you doing what you're doing?' routine. The pressure goes up and up, until someone breaks — perhaps into tears or by slamming out of the room. Either response says, in pain and anger, 'I won't play your game any longer.' One is an act of defeat, the other of rebellion and perhaps of liberation. The organizer declares the Totalitarian Classroom game ended, and asks people to talk about the experience and their feelings within it.

And its third phase begins. In the second, trapped in the game they were discussing, the players struggled with the real pain of being unable to transcend their *individual* conditioned roles. In the third, the agony continues. For, though all have now said, 'Let's stop playing this game' — and perhaps symbolized this by shifting from a classroom seating to an informal circle — they find they are playing the game still, *as a group*.

Among themselves, they can begin to discuss the experience in informal democracy. But when the organizer tries to contribute his knowledge or feelings, the geometry of control snaps back into existence. He does not want the role of Teacher any more, and says so; but the group finds with dismay that it cannot treat him otherwise, nor help him leave his very real personal imprisonment in the role.

Partly this is because they all have a large burden of anger for him that cannot be discharged by rational discussion — partly, because he still has unique expertise, and they know no other means of receiving it than by way of an Expert and in a way which reasserts totalitarian control over the group's context and process. All find that the context must be broken completely to permit a fresh start in a healthier game. From this point on, an extended workshop in learning can fruitfully proceed through a non-verbal game session dealing with the release of anger, and then into discussion and games aimed at training for an alternate style of teaching/learning interaction, radically non-authoritative and non-coercive.

A full Totalitarian Classroom takes about two hours. Well-run, it leaves its players shaken, acutely conscious of the social game structure of classroom interaction and of its destructive qualities (which are merely emphasized into visibility in T.C.). They are also left to realize that their social performance as 'good student' has little to do with whatever *being* a good learner actually means to each individual — a question which most realize they have not actually examined.

As a learning game, T.C. depends on two characteristic dissonances. The first comes from its nature as a hybrid form. Seminars proceed by intellectual reaction to intellectual process; encounter forms, by emotional response to emotional process. But T.C. proceeds by intellectual analysis of the emotional process of intellectual analysis of an emotional process. The tension or dissonance of thus combining two ways of knowing opens people to both. A similar dissonance comes from T.C.'s nature as reflexive theatre. For here the rules of the play of learning are on stage as part and focus of that play — rather than agreed upon and never mentioned, as in the theatre of the standard classroom. The players are thus forced to a doubled consciousness — within the play, and of the play *as play*, simultaneously — which painfully opens a new way of seeing.

If this bears family resemblance to, say, Brecht's theories about 'alienation' in the theatre, that is not surprising. T.C. was designed by a young English professor at the University of Illinois — Neill Kleinman — who was deeply involved with the study of modern theatre and reflexive forms. Neill played T.C. twice and described it to me. I ran three sessions as part of the Educational Reform workshop at the 1968 NSA Congress, and played and taught it on individual campuses such as Sonoma State College and Denison University. Like most of our learning games, thereafter it spread quickly and anonymously. Students at Antioch and in Pennsylvania used it to help build orientation programmes; when I visited the University of Michigan four students who had been leading T.C.'s described their individual variations; student government kids at San Diego State are practicing it upon their faculty. Its propagation testifies to its flexible strength and impact, and also to our eager need for new games and forms — of deconditioning and new creation — that will help us learn what we need to know.

Section 3. Aids to observation

We have reached a point where the kinds of analysis we have presented, and the means we have evolved for using these analyses in the construction of alternative actions, have outstretched the observational material contained in the profiles. The examples we have found ourselves using have tended to rely more and more on transcripts derived from recordings, rather than from direct observation alone, and the discussion of microteaching techniques led us to consider the use of such recording media as videotaped close-circuit television. Our understanding of classroom events is such that we now require more detailed and complex data than can easily be obtained from straightforward description. Above all our need is for methods of recording which allow us to review events in ways that retain some of their complexity and unexpectedness.

The advantage of records like those gained by using film, videotape or audiotape is that they recreate incidents more vividly than narrative description — narrative description requires understanding, insight, even theory before recording is possible. Before you can write down what you have observed you have to select, process and organize a complex array of perceptions and ideas. Use of a recording technique allows you to delay coming to an understanding; it allows you to separate out to some extent the processes involved in assimilation and accommodation.

This is not to claim that such recording techniques collect 'theory-free' data — that they record the full reality objectively. As soon as you begin to *use* such techniques you become aware of the different realities retained and created by the different techniques. The world of film is not the same as the real world — it sustains a different reality in which time and space are suggested by different conventions, and the same is true of videotape and audiotape. Much of

this section of the book is in fact about how the different realities created by alternative recording systems give them different potentials for use in the recording of classroom events.

What narrative description does convey very well is the *interpretation* of events by the observer — John Holt's anecdotes for example would not be so effective communicated by film or tape — for what is interesting about the anecdotes is the light that they throw on his total interpretation. It is not the incidents themselves that are significant but the *meanings* that they convey.

This is why we have tried to underplay the use of techniques like video recordings in these books, and to delay considering them for as long as possible. For although professionally we work more or less continuously with such techniques, we feel that the emphasis (for researchers and teachers) should always be on interpretation — on the meanings of events — not on the recordings themselves. Although many education departments and colleges now have access to equipment like videotaped close-circuit television, our impression is that in very few of them is the sophistication of the equipment matched by any imagination or understanding of the medium. The use of such techniques has great attractions, but it also involves terrible pitfalls.

Here we take a strong stand on the belief that the use of recording techniques should always be in a context of participant observation. Recordings should always be used in order to *extend* interpretation and understanding — not to replace them. They should be used as *evidence*, not as replacing the truth.

For us perhaps the most important reason for wanting to use such recordings (in teaching and research) is that they allow the sharing of experience in ways not possible with narrative description. Recordings of teachers or student teachers actually teaching provide material for understanding and discussion. For example, we have brought into a discussion group a recording of a lesson, together with the teacher concerned, as a basis for initiating discussion. We have also used recordings made during teaching practice as a source of material for the next term's discussions and activities. The important thing is to create a feeling of trust in the group so that vulnerability is not exploited, either by attack or overprotection. It is essential that whoever is recorded should feel in control of the situation — and we feel this means that whoever *uses* the recording should *make* the recording. It is no good sending out the AV unit to make recordings for you; you've got to go out and make your own.

RETAINING THE PROFILE
The use of recording techniques like tape or film does not mean relinquishing the idea of working from profiles. The profile is an index of the observer's sensitivity to changes in context within the classroom. It provides an overall descriptive and analytic framework, derived from observation, for understanding 'what happened'. Although observers' and teachers' profiles may vary in the focus of their concern, there should be considerable correspondence between them in terms of the structure of events. A useful test of proficiency is to compare your profiles with accounts elicited from teachers and pupils of the lesson you observed.

In using film or tape recordings you will often need to show only a fragment of a total recording. Here a major use for the profile is to create a context within which interpretation of the recorded fragment can be located. following are methods of recording you are most likely to

The following are methods of recording you are most likely to have some access to.

AUDIOTAPE RECORDING
In some classrooms a lot of what goes on can be captured on audiotape. Often what is *said* is a fair sample of what happens. This is not always the case, but sometimes it is. Even where there are paradoxes between what is said and what is done, it is often useful initially to present sound recordings alone to the audience — getting them to construct the situation for themselves, and *then* playing both sound and vision together.

Technical points
If there is little movement in the classroom, if most of the time only one person speaks at a time, and background noise is subdued, then an ordinary reel-to-reel or cassette tape recorder is usually adequate. (By adequate we mean it will capture enough of the talk for you to be able to understand it on playback.)

Most machines are equipped with microphones that pick up sound from all around (omnidirectional). If it is unobtrusive the microphone is best placed at a point equidistant from all speakers. If, however, the microphone is cardiod (picking up sound in a heart-shaped field — the apex being the microphone), or double-cardoid (picking up sound from a figure-of-eight-shaped field), then placement should take account of the spatial distribution of participants. There is no need to become unduly concerned with accurate placement — approximation is adequate. The problem remains, however, that placement depends on the location of people and actions in the room, not just with the acoustic qualities of the empty room, so that in order to place the microphone you need to have some idea about what is going to happen before the event, and also to be aware of any major changes in the context of activity that are likely. (If you cannot ask the teacher about the lesson then go by the furniture arrangements.)

Try to place the microphone before the event and alter it as little as possible once the lesson has begun. If you have to decide between disrupting the lesson and getting a good recording then leave things where they are. This means developing some sensitivity to the extent to which you are disrupting the lesson, which is not always as simple as it sounds.

Keep the equipment as simple as possible. Always check to see if the machine is recording before the event. If there is a lot of movement in the class then a static recorder is inadequate. Most reel-to-reel recorders are too heavy to carry around, but cassette recorders are usually small and light enough to be slung over the shoulder. The teacher may be willing to carry it around like this with the microphone fastened in front of him. As background noise in such situations is often high, the microphone should be fixed at about pupil height (not right up against the teacher's neck). It will then generally pick up most talk within a radius of about 6 feet of the teacher.

A more sophisticated but not necessarily superior solution to the problem is to use a radio microphone system. The teacher wears a small microphone connected to a pocket transmitter (little larger than a cigaretter packet). The signal is picked up by a receiver which feeds into a cassette or reel-to-reel recorder. The signal is of high quality and so can be matched by using a high quality recorder. The system is unobtrusive and simple to use, but expensive and requires careful handling. For recording in classrooms those radio microphone receivers powered by batteries are more adaptable than those requiring a mains socket.

Summary
1. Select the machine most suitable for the kind of situation you want to record. Make sure you know how it works, and after you have set it up, make sure it works, before recording.

2. Do not place omnidirectional microphones to face the teacher because the teacher's voice is almost always stronger than the children's. Even when the machine has automatic recording level it is unlikely that this will respond fast enough to pick up the fainter voices of the children.

3. Become so sure and familiar with all the devices you use that you are seen to be in control of the situation. Even when things go wrong avoid fussing over them if this creates a distraction in the lesson. Do not let the machines get between you and the situation.

We suggest the following minimal criteria for judging the quality of recordings:

1. Did you record those people and incidents that you considered crucial to your observations?
2. Can you hear what was said well enough to make a transcript of the talk through headphones?

If you want to play recordings to an audience you may need to work with better quality equipment and more care.

PHOTOGRAPHY
Sound recording selects and emphasizes sounds in ways different from those of the human listener. What you get on tape will never sound quite like what you think you heard, and what someone else gets from the tape may be quite unlike what you expect them to get. This selective distortion of reality is even more true of still photographs — they catch something quite unlike what we think we see — and yet enough like it to be recognizable and useful.

Sequences of photographs without sound recording can be used to record the physical environment of the classroom, examples of the children's work, what they look like. They can be used to document the aggregation and dissolution of groups, bottlenecks in the distribution of resources, and children's attempts to catch the teacher's attention. A set of prints or slides can be used to provide a useful context for presenting a lesson profile, but they are also part of the profile itself. The selections involved in taking photographs, in selecting and printing them are in fact judgements and hypotheses about significance — every photograph is an observation, and behind each observation is an idea being tested.

Still photographs make very good material for discussion — the interpretation of pictures often leads to alternative interpretations and so to the exploration of interesting issues. A Polaroid camera may be a useful device.

With some cameras it is possible to take time-lapse photographs. The camera is fixed and the shutter held open for a period of time. The resulting 'smearing' of the image relates the shutter speed to the speed of actions — and can be used to assess movement. The technique is useful to assess space use or gestural and body movements during discussion.

PHOTOGRAPHY WITH SOUND
The recent availability of cassette recorders with built in slide-synchronizing devices make it possible to produce tape-slide recordings of lessons relatively easily.

The technique we have devised involves the use of such a recorder (Philips 2209), a radio microphone system (Lustraphone) and a half-frame 35mm camera (Pen EE2). The participant recorder has to carry the cassette recorder, the radio microphone receiver, the synchronizing device and the camera. This sounds a lot but in practice it is more portable than the smallest videotape back-packs (e.g. Akai) and can comfortably be carried for a full school day.

The cassette recorder, loaded with a C120 cassette, is battery-driven, records continuously and automatically for one hour on one side of the tape. The camera has a fixed-focus lens and automatic exposure controls — it is loaded with high speed Ektachrome film rated at 500ASA and subsequently force-processed. The film can be bought in twenty-exposure rolls (giving forty half-frame slides) or in 100 foot rolls — when up to eighty slides can be made on one strip of film.

Our experience is that 30 to 120 photographs are taken per hour — depending on the complexity of the situation. The problem is *when* to take photographs of *what*. The method we adopt is to take pictures which illustrate the situations in which the talk is going on — the underlying question in the cameraman's mind is 'what does an outsider listening to the sound tape recording need to *see* to understand what is being said?'. The pictures show who is talking to whom, whereabouts, and what objects are being referred to. They chart increases and decreases in listeners and speakers, the introduction of new objects, changes in space use and so on, the rate depending on the fineness of the data that the observer considers may be needed.

The observer using this recording system has to be skilled at constructing profiles, and has to be able to recognize transitions with some accuracy, for while the profile can be constructed after the event, the slides have to be taken during the event.

Using this technique requires a more active observational role; inevitably you are more obtrusive in the class. On the basis of our experience we can suggest a number of rules for reference and for breaking. (Breaking the rules allows you to test impressions you may form about relationships or patterns.)

Referential rules

1. Keep out of the communication paths between teacher and children, children and children, children and resources. Generally start off on the periphery and only work your way into the group tentatively.

2. Keep the camera above or below the general level of eye contact.

3. Move into unoccupied spaces. If a large group of children move towards the teacher, move out to an open space. When the focus of activity is very small (e.g. an object on a desk) and all the children are looking at it, then any other space will be unfocused and you can work in it. When the organization becomes complex, with several focuses of attention, the participant recorder has to become like a boxer — moving into and away from others, monitoring situations continuously and attempting to predict successive actions. He has to judge and record changes in the intensity, duration and variety of activity.

As long as you can keep the lesson profile in mind you can continue to act effectively as a participant recorder, when you lose that kind of understanding you will find yourself having difficulties with self location and unobtrusiveness.

An example might help clarify some of the points raised so far:

The teacher is talking to a group of eight primary school children about a collection of rocks and minerals on a table. She describes them and then gives them to the pupils for examination. Fifteen other pupils — the rest of the class — are sitting doing mainly small-group seatwork with workcards. The participant recorder is photographing the focus of activity around the teacher — he is not impassive but responds to pupil glances and even makes comments about the crystals like 'that's lovely', 'I like that'; meanwhile he is able to monitor the group for changes in activity in order to anticipate a photograph.

The teacher holds up a large quartz crystal 'from Brazil'. She asks the children about it and hands it around. Some of the children are more interested in it than others, who tend to pass it on the the next or to those who are more enthusiastic. Eventually one boy holds the crystal up to the light and accidentally obtains some wedge-shaped rainbows on the ceiling. Some of the group are still looking at the other minerals. The teacher comments to the boy holding the quartz — 'that's interesting'. Then he leaves the group, goes to the far end of the room and gradually other children aggregate round him in order to try their hands at 'making rainbows' — these are children who were previously doing seatwork. The participant recorder sees this as the creation of a new focus of activity, but delays moving from his established space with the group until he can judge the level of interest and transience of the new group. After a while about ten 'seatwork' children are gathered around the crystal. Photographs are being taken mainly side-on to this group. The teacher is aware that the main focus of activity has shifted from her group, although the crystal is, as it were, a portmanteau for a context she does have control over. She tells the boy to return to her group, and as an aside to the recorder says 'sorry about that — it sometimes happens'.

In the routine of this classroom this is an 'unusual' or at least a problematic event. It is interesting that what creates a problem for the participant recorder is also soon seen as a problem by the teacher. In other words the recorder's 'profile' of the incident must be very similar to the teacher's. In other classrooms, where there are continuously more focuses of activity and a wider variety of tasks, resources and spaces being used, the problems for the recorder become daunting. He either has to attempt to pursue particular interpretations, hypotheses, people or incidents, or to use more complex recording strategies involving the use of

Reviewing the tape-slide sequences

The sequence is basically a sound recording, supplemented and filled in at critical points by visual illustration. To interpret the sequence means *listening to what is said* more intently than you would with either videotape or regular movie film. The presentation makes strong demands on the audience in terms of both concentration and interpretation. Videotaped close-circuit television gives continuous visual information at low definition; slides give high definition images at intervals. It follows that slides emphasize context and situation much more than videotape — relative to television, slides de-emphasize the person, but accentuate the situation.

TELEVISION

(Here we have ignored technical questions — to anyone interested in pursuing these we strongly recommend the CATS Manual*.)

Video-recording systems range from 'simple' one-camera, narrow gauge systems to highly complicated multi-camera systems. *Our emphasis here is on naturalistic recording, not on programme-making.* For the participant recorder, complex, complicated systems are likely to produce less good, relevant material than simpler systems. The ground rule we adopt is to choose recording systems which produce material of a kind that matches *both* the complexity of the situation and the complexity of the ideas being used to interpret the situation. It follows that sophisticated systems (multi-camera, multi-sound source recordings with cutting facilities etc.) will only be used — for recording as opposed to

*Centre for Advanced Television Studies, 15 Prince of Wales Crescent, London NW1 (editors: Kirk and Hopkirk).

programme-making — when the observer is highly ignorant, or when he is concerned with very fine-grained, contextual analyses.

Videotaped television has two distinct advantages over the systems described already: one is the possibility of instant replay of sound and image; the other is recording of movement in real time exactly synchronized with sound. Although this second point may be a real advantage in some situations, it does have disadvantages.

1. One is that the participant recorder has to concentrate on following activities *through* the experience of the camera rather than *using* the camera to document what he sees for himself. In order to get acceptable images he has to think in terms of when to zoom, focus, pan, tilt, track etc. He sees the situation *through* the camera rather than *with* the camera (the medium becomes the message). This is especially true when multi-camera set-ups are being used and the observer is actually outside the classroom surveying an array of monitors and manipulating a cutting-box — the participant function is virtually absent and the observer is unable to use himself as a research instrument.

2. In using television it is extremely easy to become dominated by the conventions of programme-making. For example, television programmes tend to have most impact when close-up shots are liberally used. If the cameraman or director of classroom recordings follows this convention and moves into close-up or ultra close-up at almost every opportunity he will create an image which may destroy the record required for observation. The participant recorder's concern will generally be with situations and contexts; with who is *listening* as much as with who is *talking*; with the growth and decay of focus of activity, not simply with the focus itself. Close-up shots will rarely be useful — the convention might almost be reformulated to say that the participant recorder frames shots with as *wide* an angle as

possible, because his concern will be with the limits and boundaries of attention rather than with their focus.

We mention these points here because television is often used for recording and replay rather uncritically. It is not always the most appropriate method to use, and the images it presents are open to criticism, for it necessarily incorporates in its methods a *view* of events as well as a record. It is as much *a way of looking at* events in classrooms as it is a way of recording them.

Videotaped television is good for recording non-oral aspects of communication, both of speakers and listeners, but even 'back-packs' tend to be obtrusive and tiring to manage for long sessions and so their use is restricted to relatively short time-samples. Perhaps the most useful facility the method provides is the possibility of instant playback — for example in microteaching sessions.

MOVIE FILM
Even 8mm film is expensive (and unlike videotape cannot be rubbed out and used again). Synchronization of sounds is complicated, the film is delicate, and may be 'eaten' by projectors. 16mm movie film is beyond the budget and expertise of most observers, and rarely a relevant method for use in naturalistic recordings rather than programme-making. Nevertheless, in the hands of professionals it is a remarkable observational recording instrument (see for example the film 'School' in BBC Television's *Space Between Words* series). The use of film in this way requires considerable skill in predicting, interpreting and reconstructing patterns of events. Prior to the filming, decisions have to be made about the overall stucture of the film and perhaps an outline or script produced; during filming judgements are made by cameramen, and by sound recordists about how to selectively record incidents; and after recording the whole event has to be recreated by an editor. The director has to control all three phases of production in order to realize a finished film which relates both to the original event and to his own understanding of it.

16 mm STOP-FRAME RECORDING
During 1970—2 we were engaged in a study of 'open' classrooms which demanded some sort of audio-visual recording technique for observing the teachers at work. An example of the kind of recording problem we faced was an open-plan science laboratory designed to house 120 pupils at a time with up to four teachers (plus student teachers, technicians and remedial specialists), off which were five smaller teaching areas whose occupants traversed the central area throughout the lesson.

To investigate minimally this situation required two people acting as participant observers and recorders. We did not want to use a multi-camera close-circuit television set-up because this demands instantaneous cutting, which is only possible when you know precisely what you want to record. We did not know what was worth recording except in retrospect and so had to preserve the records of each camera.

The system we devised consisted of two 16mm recording cameras, which ran for four hours each on 200 ft of film. As we were using high speed colour film we did not require additional lighting and got images which were considerably more detailed than those obtained by most television systems. One camera (with a zoom lens) was usually manned, the other had a fixed-focus wide-angle lens which covered the whole scene from a position high up over the action. Photographs were taken automatically at intervals of two seconds (one second in some classrooms, especially primary ones). The film was synchronized with sound using similar principles to tape-slide presentation.

REPLAYING THE IMAGES

Like others who have used visual recordings to capture human communication, we find that the continuously moving image (on film or videotape) encourages the audience to identify with the actions — especially when the material is presented in programme form. In contrast, stop-frame film and slide sequences retain more strongly their identity as visual representations — in that sense they are less convincing than the continuously moving image. This means that the viewers have to work to fill in and remedy the spaces between the images — using what information they can gain from the talk. In practice this means that showing a slide sequence to an audience immediately creates bases for interpretation and discussion which are *not* generally provided by film or videotape. This gives such methods of recording unique uses, both in research and in teacher education, for those who are aware of their potential. They are not simply substitutes or cheaper or simpler techniques for film or television, but open up new areas of inquiry which users of the continuously moving image generally have failed to realize.*

CHOOSING AN APPROPRIATE RECORDING SYSTEM
Tape recordings
Audio tape recordings are ideal when the situation and setting present no problems of interpretation. Formal classrooms, discussion groups and small groups within informal classrooms all generally record well and provide useful tapes.**

*See for example, Biddle and Adams, *The Realities of the Classroom* (Holt, Rinehart and Winston, 1970).
**It is not always true that situations involving *things* rather than words record badly — witness some of Charles Parker's Radio Ballads and the recent radio documentaries by Tony van der Bergh about modern surgical techniques.

Tape/slide
Can be used in all situations but particularly useful in informal situations with several focuses of activity.

Movie film
Regular movie film: for very specific aspects of situations — for example, studies of one child, or of a small group of children with a resource being rapidly manipulated so that the film can be looped in order to view the sequence again and again.

High speed movie film: for fine-grained analyses of movement — e.g. facial expressions.

Time lapse: for studies of the intensity of space use.

Stop-frame; for visually sampling activities at selected rates.

Television
For discussions, for details of particular interactions in formal and informal classrooms. When instant replay is required (e.g. in microteaching, role-play or simulation exercises). (Note such facilities as time lapse are now available on some television systems.)

WHEN YOU HAVE GOT THE RECORDING, WHAT DO YOU DO WITH IT?
This brief account of available recording methods has been set in a context of developing observational skills that can be related to action. But having developed the skill for constructing lesson profiles and for documenting the contexts within which to understand them, there are other, simpler but more sophisticated methods that may sometimes be useful. These are ususally referred to as 'checklists and category systems'. Some checklists and category systems can be used only with recordings, some with both recordings and

'live'. There is a full description of the different methods available (*Mirrors for Behaviour* ed. Boyer and Simon) — the total runs to over 100.

Checklists consist of lists of items that may be found in classrooms. The observer simply ticks these off if he sees them in a particular setting during a set time period.* Tested checklists are available, but they are mostly old, American and little used.**

Informal lists of limited use are easily constructed and may be of some use when applied by a group of students in different schools or classes. The material contained in the 'Observation handbook' could easily act as a resource for anyone wanting to start constructing a list.

*D. M. Medley and H. E. Mitzel, *Oscar* (a combined checklist and category system) includes the items:

1. Teacher lectures
2. Teacher reads, tells story
3. Teacher talks to class
4. Teacher illustrates at boards etc.

1. Pupil talks to group
2. Pupil reads aloud
3. Pupil sings, plays instrument
4. Pupil plays game
5. Pupil scuffles, fidgets
6. Pupil whispers
7. Pupil laughs
8. Pupil talks to visitor etc.

1. Use of blackboard
2. Use of slides, film
3. Special teaching aid etc.

**D. M. Medley and H. E. Mitzel, 'Measuring classroom behaviour by systematic observation', in *Handbook of Research on Teaching*, ed. N. L. Gage, (Rand McNally, 1963).

The difference between an informal checklist and the kind of professional checklists described by Medley and Mitzel lies in the significance that can be attached to the data. Professional checklists should have been thoroughly tested for reliability — and the items included not simply because they 'seem' significant, but because they have been *shown* to be significant to a calculated precision.

Checklists consist of a relatively large number of descriptive items which can be statistically reduced to a manageable (and meaningful) form. Category systems consist of a small number of items which can be recorded in such a way that relative quantities within the categories are significant. A checklist, when used in any one classroom, will have a large number of blank spaces, since part of the description the checklist provides is of things that do *not* happen in that class, but which do happen in others. A category system usually considers only those items which occur in all classrooms, but finds significance in the *extent* to which (or sequence in which) they happen in any one classroom.

It will be clear from the descriptions we have given that checklists and category systems are essentially for studying variations between classrooms, rather than variations within classrooms. One category system, however, has been developed to a point where it can be used for studying one classroom. This is Ned Flander's system of interaction analysis. The clearest description of this system is to be found in Flander's own book, *Studying Teaching Behaviour* (Wiley, 1971). A useful development of the method in teacher education is Amidon and Hunter's *Improving Teaching* (Holt, Rinehart and Winston, 1966). A considerable advantage of Flander's method is that it allows the analysis of certain talk strategies, and gives teachers means of knowing when they have controlled, or failed to control, the tactics underlying these strategies. The method is, though, only useful in certain kinds of classroom situation, particularly formal situations.

THREE ADDITIONAL METHODS

Three further methods are worth considering in studying teaching — interviewing, sociometry and constructs. These each provide information which can be used to elucidate and extend redordings

Interviewing

Through interviews common motives, intentions and interpretations which can usually only be inferred from recordings may be revealed.

In practice this means that multiple interviews are required with all the participants in order to uncover different points of view and their relation to role, status or task differences. These interviews would attempt to reveal particularly the perceptions each participant had of the other's actions.

Not only should interviews be multiple, and an attempt made to cross-reference statements and perceptions — but key participants (e.g. the teacher) may be interviewed both before and after the event.

Subsequent interviews are usually best made by replaying an extract from the recording that seems to raise problems for interpretation for you or for outsiders. Alternatively the whole recording can be replayed and participants' comments used as a way of trying to find what is problematic for them. A set of interviews made around a recording may be as follows:

1. teacher's brief statement before lesson about what he plans to do
2. teacher's response to the lesson immediately after the event

3. interview with teacher on seeing recording
4. interview with children involved in particular events
5. (4) may be played back to teacher and used as a basis for a further interview.

Further exploration may be useful (both to teacher and observer) but this is usually sufficient and leads to people beginning to repeat themselves or saying 'stop!'.

Managing to be an interviewer

Unlike the kind of interviews usually used by social scientists you are likely to be perceived by the participants less as an interviewer and more as a witness to the event. Usually interviewers ask about events they have not observed; you will be asking for their view of events you have both observed, and you may both have recorded evidence available for reference. This gives you a relationship unlike the usual interview relationship which you may have to learn to manage.

In general interviews are unstructured at the start (even uninitiated), but tend to become more structured as time goes on. The interviewer can structure interviews to some extent by the selections he makes (of incidents for replay for example).

Each question you ask should be simple and have a single purpose. The reply will direct or constrain your next question. Some aspects you will be able to deal with in a straightforward way ('Did they use the workcards last week?'). Some answers might provide opportunities for cross-referencing with something said before, or somethg else you have observed in the classroom or in interviews.

There are always many possible research strategies you *might* adopt — children can interview children, teachers can interview children, children can interview teachers . . .

Talking to children in unstructured interviews is very similar to talking to them in informal, personal classrooms. The same relationship, based on equal rights to speak and change topics, exists. The following guidelines from the American curriculum project *Man: A Course of Study** may be helpful.

A new role

An enjoyable and important aspect of interviewing is that the classroom teacher can step back from the demands of the teaching role and become a learner, a listener. There are occasions in the classroom when the teacher can listen to children without 'monitoring' their ideas. But in the interview the teacher does no 'teaching', makes no corrections, suggests no further examples or illustrations, passes no judgement on the mode of presentation. It is a time when children can 'tell it like it is'.

Attentive listening and questioning produce the best interviews, when children reveal the full range of their thinking and feeling. Children of this age when asked for opinions, when asked to judge materials, when asked to clarify ideas, usually respond with great zest. They care a great deal about being treated as 'grown-ups', about displaying competence and about showing their grasp of a subject area — in fact, they often show an assimilation of detail that is awe-inspiring.

Introducing the interview

The teacher must put the children as much at ease as possible. An atmosphere unlike that of a traditional classroom test helps draw out the best ideas that children have. One way to create the relaxed mood is for the interviewer to introduce himself in his new role thus:

When you work in groups or when discussions are going

**Evaluation Strategies*, 1970.

on, I don't get as good an opportunity as I'd like to hear the ideas and opinions of each of you. So I thought that occasionally we could gather in small groups so that you could talk about the course. I'd like to hear more of your personal opinions. I'd also like to hear your thoughts about some of the ideas of this course. Many of them are very new and not always easy at first. Maybe you can help me to understand what ideas you personally don't find clear, and what you think we need to spend more time or less time doing.

Mechanics of the interview

We suggest that children be interviewed in groups of three or four for about twenty minutes while the rest of the class pursue other activities. You might interview two groups in one day, spreading the interviews over a week or more, Or you might decide to interview only half the class after the Animals section and the rest after the Netsilik* section. (Children will want to be told this, if you so decide.) An area apart from the classroom is best for interviewing; if that is not available, then the quietest corner or the section of the room furthest from the rest of the class is the best, alternative, with the children sitting with you in a small circle and facing away from the class.

As you start each interview, some simple explanation of procedure may be necessary. Children should know that this is not a time for raising hands — this is a chance to talk among themselves, and discuss the questions put to them. As long as they speak one at a time, there are no fixed rules of procedure — just a normal flow of conversation.

The primary function of the interviewer is to set the stage and control the pace of the conversation. During the interview, there should be no correction of children's statements. Often, the children correct each other, but the

*The Netsilik are a group of Eskimo studied in detail on the course.

listener should (however difficult it may be) refrain from 'teaching'.

To avoid the problem of the child who wants to monopolize the interview, it should be made clear that each student has a turn at answering a question (with elaborations following from the rest of the group), and that the amount of interview time is limited. In this way the interviewer also gets a clearer sense of the personal knowledge and attitudes of each child.

You may want to have a few sets of questions that you alternate among groups so that a new kind of 'test-wiseness' doesn't take over. Perhaps one or two of the questions you feel are most important could be common to all interviews.

The interviewer should keep an interested but unevaluative expression (if possible) so that children will not perceive what he wants or expects to hear.

Summary of interviewing pointers
1. Children must feel relaxed and at ease with the interviewer-teacher, to the point where they feel free to say what they really think (or feel) about a given subject without fear of criticism or correction. Be as encouraging, reassuring and supportive as possible without influencing or biasing the content of what the student is saying.

   a. Be a *sympathetic, interested* and *attentive* listener, without taking an active conservative role; this is a way of conveying that you value and appreciate the child's opinion.
   b. Be *neutral* with respect to subject matter. Do not express your own opinions either on the subjects being discussed by the children or on the children's ideas about these subjects, and be especially careful not to betray feelings of surprise or disapproval at what the child knows.

   c. Your own sense of ease is also important. If you feel hesitant or hurried, the student will sense this feeling and behave accordingly.
   d. The students may also be fearful that they will expose an attitude or idea that you don't think is correct. Reassure along the lines of 'Your opinions are important to me. All I want to know is just whatever you think — this isn't a test and there isn't any one answer to the questions I want to ask.'

2. Specifically we suggest that you

   a. phrase each question similarly each time
   b. keep the outline of interview questions before you
   c. be prepared to reword a question if it is not understood or if the answer is vague and too general. Sometimes it is hard not to give an 'answer' to the question in the process of rewording it.

3. Eliciting full and relevant responses is perhaps the most challenging aspect of interviewing — the facet of the task requiring the most patience and skill. The general technique for solving these problems is called 'probing' — or *continued neutral questioning*.
Don't knows. Children sometimes understandably use a 'don't know' response to gain some time to gather their thoughts. Don't be in too big a rush to move to another question. If you sit quietly — but expectantly — students will usually think of something further to say. Silence and waiting are frequently your best probes for a 'don't know'. You'll also find that other useful probes are: 'Well what do you think?' 'I just want your ideas on that.' After a reasonable length of time, however, simply go on to another question.

4. To summarize: in the interview situation, which is probably somewhat unique to children, your job is to *help* the child give answers which are relevant, clear and complete

as he is capable of making them. This is not an occasion to pass judgements or opinions or to clear up misconceptions. Finally, if you wish, jot down or record at the end of the interview anything about the manner, reactions and non-verbal gestures of the children that may have bearing on their answers to specific topics.

Examples of good and bad interview questions
While in the process of evaluating students' responses, it is wise to keep in mind that the way in which a question is posed affects the nature of the response. Following are examples of ways in which questions might be formed, with some comments as to their effectiveness.

Questions on materials

Poor	Did you enjoy the film on the chimpanzee?	Allows for one-word rather than in-depth response. 'Enjoy' is leading word — generally precludes possibility of negative response.
Better	How did the film on the chimpanzee compare with the other films you have seen so far?	Question sets up problem which can then be dealt with by child in whichever way he chooses — responses will often be content-oriented.

Questions on content

Poor	What is innate behaviour?	Asked in isolation, this question requires definition as response. Sets up test-like (and threatening) situation.
Better	How would you explain to someone the difference between innate and learned behaviour?	Requires contrast and comparison rather than definition and puts the child in a responsible role.
Poor	Is pecking an innate behaviour of a herring gull?	Asks for straight recall.
Better	If someone said to you that human and herring gull parents are very much alike, what would you say?	Sets up a problem to which most students will readily react. Comparative illustrations sought. Less test-like in tone. Could then be followed by a more direct question, such as 'What do you mean by innate behaviour?' should the student himself use the term.

Questions on attitude toward Netsilik

Poor	In what ways is the Netsilik family like yours?	Leading question — assumes that there are similarities.
Better	Does the Netsilik family seem like your family in any way?	Permits the child to decide whether or not he sees similarities.
Poor	Now that you have seen a number of films on the Netsilik do you admire them or dislike them.	Forces the child to take a side.
Better	Did you see any film that made you admire the Netsilik? Did you see any film that made you dislike them?	Allows for evaluations on both dimensions.

SOCIOMETRY

Several books, of different standards of difficulty, are available on sociometric techniques. Basically sociometric surveys allow you to map the relationships children say they have with each other. Their use in this context is that they allow you to relate what children *say* to what they *do* (as revealed by the recordings.) This may provide starting points for interview or further study. For example, we have sometimes pursued the idea that with some teachers and in some subjects, children in informal classes mobilize their friendship networks as a way of reducing their vulnerability to the teacher.

Again we stress — take care with sociometric surveys. Do not, as one student did, pin them on the classroom wall; unless you really know what you are doing. Take advice on how to use them, if possible discuss why you are using them with the children and never let the method dominate your concern to the exclusion of your ideas and intentions.

CONSTRUCTS

Constructs venture even further into what may be (or become) delicate areas. Use them with care. Constructs aim to depict people's characteristic meanings. They were devised by the American psychologist George Kelly as a simple effective method of assessing change in individual patients. He postulated that each person has a set of constructs with which he accounts for his experiences of the world.

The theory has been elaborated, refined and operationalized in various ways and there has been some incisive criticism of it.* A simple technique to elicit an individual's constructs is to provide three names of people known to the respondent (say of pupils) and ask the question, 'Think of some important way in which any two of them seem to be alike and to contrast to the third.'

*R. Holland.

142

The respondent eventually yields a pair of contrasting terms ('dimensions'). The pairing is called the 'construct'. For instance, 'One is lazy, the other two are hardworking.' The terms are usually vernacular expressions but often have particular collections of meanings for each person. Thus *lazy — hardworking* for one teacher will not contain the same nuances of meaning for another teacher. Another danger for the researcher is to equate the *mental lazy* with the *physical lazy*. Certainly there can be no combination of one person's constructs with another's unless the meanings of terms used to express the construct are identicial — and that is extremely difficult to demonstrate.* However when related to participant observation and interviews 'constructs' may provide additional insight into why one teacher has a particular relationship with individual pupils and another teacher a different one. Of course all relationships are reciprocal so pupils' constructs of the teachers should also be elicited. If more than one teacher is familiar with a pupil, a comparison of each teacher's constructs and their individual rank order may be revealing, in relation to prior observation, recording and interviews of these teachers with that pupil.

We have based two methods on the notion of constructs: having elicited 'dimensions' during informal discussions with groups of teachers about the practice of inquiry/discovery teaching, we sent the collection of contrasting terms to individual teachers. They rated themselves and other colleagues on a one to seven scale. Two aspects emerged — that the terms were 'real' to the teachers and could be cross-checked, e.g. consistently similar ratings on the polar pairs, authoritarian/democratic, open-ended/guided.

These responses seem to indicate the similarity in meaning of these terms for teachers — at least within the school teams That the terms have shared meanings enables us to be a little more certain that changes in rating of self and others would

*See Frake.

arise from changes in the sort of knowledge each teacher has of the others. Some dimensions may change little, even across schools. These would presumably be those called 'impermeable' by Kelly. The second way we have applied the 'construct' hypothesis is to provide a method of monitoring change additional to interview recording and participant observation and the teacher's own research.*

*See Ford Teaching Project.

Appendix 1. A selection of discussion material

We have found this selection of ten pieces of evidence useful in discussion as a way of checking on the ideas we have pursued in this book. We have used it towards the end of courses as a way of evaluating our progress with the group. Other people may wish to use it as a basis for adding more material but we feel that this selection cuts through to some of the issues underlying the ideas we have presented here.

SYNOPSIS OF MATERIAL

1. An account by Willard Waller of how pupils initiate and sustain social distance from the teacher

2. An account by Willard Waller of some strategies which initiate and sustain a particular relationship with the pupil. This relationship is then the context into which 'knowledge is introduced'

3. Different interpretations of photographs

4. Three transcripts illustrating some common teacher talk strategies

5. Students discuss some problems inherent in how to start a discussion including the 'silent' pupil

6. The physical environment and its constraints on discussion and the role of the teacher in discussion

7. This extract discusses some of the practical implications for the teacher and pupils of inquiry-based learning

8. This extract from *Culture Against Man* by Jules Henry concerns the unintended concomitants of attempts at communication

9. This extract from *Culture Against Man* by Jules Henry illustrates that a 'conventional' teaching strategy can often inhibit 'trying' on the pupil's behalf. Henry believes that this example illustrates the 'failure' syndrome

10. Problems about the chicken's egg.

1. PUPIL DISTANCE: BUFFER PHRASES

Students in their turn have ways of fending off undue advances from teachers. The young have their reserves which they rarely cast off in the presence of their elders, and likewise the subordinate has an inner life into which only his equals can penetrate. Defences of the young against the teacher's curiosity and occasional yearning to be accepted by students consist mainly in treating the teacher as a teacher and refusing to consider him otherwise. Many a teacher attempting to make his classes personal has felt the disgust of certain reserved members of his classes, and not a few have been called to order by some quiet and respectful student who wanted to ask a question about the lesson. The respect of students disciplines the teacher. It is important for the teacher to know that social distance, unless it is to be quite destructive of the self-respect of the subordinated person, must always have two sides. If the teacher is to maintain his own reserves he must respect those of his students.

But it is not enough for teachers to know how to keep their students at a distance. They must know how to control the impact of their personalities upon students (and the impact of students' personalities upon themselves) in such a way as to avoid giving unnecessary hurt to the sensitive, to obviate antagonism, to arouse the interest of students, and to draw them into the social process in which learning takes place. We turn to an analysis of the mechanisms, revolving around the use of set phrases, and conventionalized verbal formulae, by which these social manipulations are accomplished.

Persons engaged in certain kinds of salesmanship are coached in the proper use of what are known as buffer phrases. These are phrases to be used when an objection has been made to the programme one is trying to promote, or when a question has been raised that one does not care to answer or is not prepared to answer at that time. The buffer phrases which are then interjected into the conversation are phrases which seem to have come in quite naturally, but which enable the salesman to gain time to think or to divert the attention of the person from the point he was making. Everyone uses phrases in this way to gain time, or uses noises made with his voice for that purpose, but buffer phrases enable one to think for a second while one appears to be taking up the conversation where the other person left off. Phrases which can be used to gain time are such expressions as the following: 'Well, now I'll tell you about that, Mrs Jones', 'Well, Mr Smith, it's this way,' 'It's just like this, Mr Hopper,' 'You see, Mr Johnson, it's this way', etc. Phrases which can be used to gain time and also to divert attention from the issue, or to postpone its consideration until it is forgotten or taken up in a different connection are such as the following: 'Now that is a good point, Mr Jones, and I am very glad indeed that you brought that up . . .', 'I was coming to that, Mrs Smith', or 'We'll come to that in just another minute, Mrs Smith.'

Teachers are not under the same sort of pressure as the salesman, but they often have need of buffer phrases. On occasion, teachers learn to apply all these devices and many more. Probably it is better, and certainly it is more honest, for the teacher who is perplexed to take time to think, and if he thinks of no adequate answer, to confess his ignorance frankly and promise to remedy it. But not all teachers are temperamentally constituted to wait five seconds between the time a question is put and the time when they begin to answer it, and as they require rapid-fire answers of others they likewise require them of themselves; further, the social situation of the classroom does not always permit of deliberation, and many teachers do not feel that it ever permits a frank confession of ignorance. Therefore teachers use buffer phrases to gain time and to conceal ignorance. They use all the phrases mentioned above, and in addition they have some of their own which have a great ring of verisimilitude. They say, 'Let us not anticipate, John. That will come a little later in the course'; 'Now when I get through talking I think you will understand that all right'; 'I think we had better stick to the lesson, John. Now what were the issues in the presidential campaign of 1832?'

There are other sorts of phrases which are used in a similar manner but which do not merit so cynical a presentation. They are sometimes used to gain time, too, but the time which they seemingly waste is required for transition, and beneath their apparent waste is a real achievement in maintaining a friendly tone and avoiding antagonistic rapport. They are buffer phrases because they are rather artificially interjected into the conversation, and because they postpone the actual statement of the teacher's opinion or enable him to hide his actual attitude. But the dissembling in them is the dissembling of one who chooses to reveal himself gradually in order to be the more fairly evaluated, and the time that such words waste is time that is needed for the other person to change his mind. Artificial they are, certainly, but an artificiality of speech that enables another to retire gracefully from an erroneous position is justifiable. Getting along with people is mainly saving their faces.

In the simplest case, the teacher uses certain quite formalized and artificial phrases to crystallize the interest of the student and to gain a further rapport with him. One says, 'That's a very good point, and I am glad you brought that up. It deserves serious consideration'. In a discipline such as sociology, it is often possible to reply with perfect honesty to a student question in this wise: 'Yes, Mr Jones, that is a good question, and I am glad it occurs to you because it shows that you are doing some thinking of your own. It is one of the great unsolved questions of human nature (or of social organization). I imagine that many of us in this line of work have been puzzled by it at one time or another. Now my opinion is . . . (directly contrary to that of the student).'

If one wishes to go further with such a technique, and to take advantage of the opportunity thus afforded to impart information, advance an argument, or instil a favourable attitude, one may use the question as a means of catching hold of the student. This is done through the use of the technique of persuasion. One says, as above,

'Yes, Mr Jones, that is a good question. It covers an important point, etc. Your question seems to reflect a certain point of view, which I believe could be stated in this way . . . Now that is a very tenable point of view, and one for which many arguments may be advanced. It is vastly superior to the unenlightened attitude which holds that . . . At one time I was strongly committed to your present point of view. Many able students of society still think that way. Their arguments are very convincing, and I believe that those arguments are perfectly sound as far as they go. The principal arguments are . . . Those are excellent arguments, and I can see how they convince many persons. To me, they seem to fall down, or to fail to be entirely convincing, because they leave out of consideration certain other important matters (or certain facts, or certain emphases indicated by modern researches). But a few years ago we all believed that (feeble-mindedness was a principal cause of crime). It seemed reasonable, and it looked as if it were true. But So-and-So came along and proved conclusively that, according to the army tests, there was the same percentage of feeble-mindedness in the general population as was revealed by the same tests in the prisons. The inference from that, you see, is pretty unmistakable, if we are to believe that the tests really test intelligence, which they may not do . . . This conclusion was corroborated by other investigations which showed the same result. Now we are almost forced to believe that we must look elsewhere for the fundamental cause of crime.'

(From *The Sociology of Teaching* by Willard Waller (Wiley, 1932).

2. SOCIAL DISTANCE

Social distance is characteristic of the personal entanglements of teachers and students. It is a necessity where the subordination of one person to another is required, for distance makes possible that recession of feeling without which the authority of another is not tolerable. Students would hate teachers more than they do if it were not for the fact that distance between the teacher and his students makes the teacher relatively meaningless as a person.

A certain social distance is necessary even where students and teacher have made the transition from secondary group contacts to primary group contacts where long use has metamorphosed a categorical into a personal contact. For the only primary group attitudes which are compatible with dominance and subordination are those which grow up within the relationship itself. All primary group attitudes established on a purely personal basis, without the one party insisting upon or the other accepting the authority of the teacher, are likely to come into conflict with the schoolroom relationship. But if the primary group attitudes spring up within the situation as defined in terms of dominance and subordination they do not cause the teacher's authority to be questioned. Primary group attitudes born of experience on the playground may indeed enhance the prestige of the teacher: if the teacher performs favourably in any respect, they may enhance it much; in other cases a situation of contradiction and re-enforcement is established. But it should be borne in mind that the intimate association of teachers and students in play, whereby primary group attitudes sometimes arise to humanize the teacher-pupil relation, is possible only by virtue of the acceptance of social distance.

Between adult and child is an irreducible social distance that seems at times an impassable gulf. The distance arises from the fact that the adult has absorbed the heritage of the group, and represents therefore in some sense the man plus the wisdom of all his ancestors, whereas the child is much more the natural and uncultivated man, and from the fact that the adult has found his place in the world and the child has not. The distance arising from these facts is but little diminished when the adult is in revolt against the group heritage which he has assimilated or when he is not satisfied with the place which he has attained in the world. To the natural distance between adult and child is added a greater distance when the adult is a teacher and the child is a student, and this distance arises mainly from the fact that the teacher must give orders to the child; they cannot know each other, for we can never know a person at whom we only peer through institutional bars. Formality arises in the teacher-pupil relationship as a means of maintaining social distance, which in its turn is a means to discipline.

Almost every teacher has certain favourite means whereby he maintains the necessary distance between himself and his students. These means are usually a part of the teacher's personality, and are the function of his general social adjustment, so that they are applied without any awareness of their effect, or with only a vague realization that 'one must keep one's place'. They are, for all that, none the less effective. Most important of the means whereby distance is maintained, and most closely connected with the teacher's personality, is that classroom procedure which defines the situation in an impersonal manner and excludes possibilities of spontaneous human interaction. This is the dry,

matter-of-fact, formal procedure of the classroom, a human intercourse which gives nothing and asks nothing of personalities but is always directed at the highly intellectualized matter to be studied. Spontaneous human intercourse is often inconsequential and meandering; it goes first here and then there as the various attitudes of persons are called out and in turn call out relevant attitudes of others, but classroom intercourse must always more or less follow the custom, the outline, and the book. If it is rarely interesting it is bearable because it is impersonal. If it is rarely inspired, it is not so often silly and absurd as it would be if it followed the whims of human beings who are absurd and silly. It is an intercourse which gives nothing of the self and reveals nothing of it but contrariwise does not demand anything of it. The teacher questions, the pupils answer. The pupils question, the teacher answers. The teacher assigns tasks, the pupils do them. The pupils do lessons, the teacher criticizes. Occasionally there comes a temptation to wander from the path beaten deep by the generations. The teacher, mindful of the course of study, brings the class back to the matter in hand for the day. This is the most effective and the most painless means by which the teacher maintains social distance between himself and his charges. As shoptalk has it, 'he lets them know that he means business'.

For many teachers a businesslike teaching manner is all that is required to fend off possible advances from students which might lead to a diminution of the social distance between teacher and student. Other teachers have worked out, not wholly consciously, techniques by which approaches may be discouraged and the teacher protected from intimate contact with students. A favoured technique is to answer all statements regarded as improper for a teacher to receive from students in a cold voice and in words distinctly non-committal. Teacher and student are talking in a friendly but still distant way; the student is moved to a burst of confidence and he remarks, 'I sure was out on a swell date last night.' The teacher answers, 'How interesting', and passes on to another subject. Or a student comes to a teacher with a complaint about another teacher. The teacher answers, 'I feel quite sure Mr So-and-So is competent to run his classes.' The tone is dry, uninterested, and disapproving. There is likewise a look which betokens social distance, and reminds the offender of the difference in the formal positions of the persons concerned. In a moment of friendliness and familiarity, the student lays his hand upon the teacher's shoulder. Turning, retracting his head, and gently desengaging himself from the contact, the teacher remarks in a frigid manner, 'Oh, yes, Mr Jackson.' Or a student assumes in class a bit too relaxed a position, or seems slightly too free with his opinions, and the teacher looks at him coldly and at once looks away. The favourite technique of college teachers who wish to discourage expression of student opinions is to listen to such expressions politely, and then to say, 'Hum! Yes! Are there any other contributions?' accompanying the words with a bored look and a slight but evident straining to be polite. It should be noted too that the look of animosity with which teachers occasionally quell students who are guilty of misconduct is a look which asserts the existence of an immense social distance, a look which says, 'You are a very low form of creation. Between you and me there is no human bond. The distance is so great that I can look at you with the most unrestrained animosity.'

There are many other techniques which are used for the purpose of re-establishing social distance. One is the interposition of a command or a fault-finding assertion in a situation which the teacher believes is becoming too intimate. The teacher has unbent somewhat and the student is alarmingly at ease. Gently the teacher reminds him of the the formal relationship: 'Now, John, I want you to have that Latin lesson tomorrow.' Or the teacher says, with friendly roughness, 'Now don't let me hear any more bad reports from you', or, 'Now see to it that you keep up your record, or I'll be right after you.' Less adroitly, she says 'These papers show that you have not been applying yourself, John. I'm afraid you are a very careless boy.' A certain college professor who often unbends in private saves himself partially from a carryover of familiarity by referring at the end of the conference to school matters and taking the opportunity to deliver certain teacher-orientated bits of advice and criticism. It is a technique which represents an excellent compromise between intimacy and authority. It is friendliness without a complete abdication of distance and the authoritative role. If the familiarity which the student is displaying is of a sort more dangerous and there are no desirable attitudes to be carried over from the situation, the teacher sometimes uses tactics less polite. She says, 'Please don't lean over my desk when you are talking to me', or, 'Stand up straight. Don't slop over so; now what is it you came up here to say? In other cases the teacher meets some bit of self-revelation on the part of the student with the definite statement that he is not interested and a reminder of the strictly business relationship existing between the two.

(From *The Sociology of Teaching* by Willard Waller (Wiley, 1932).)

3. DIFFERENT INTERPRETATIONS OF PHOTOGRAPHS

Boy: This is a piece which I brought up. At the Royal College of Art also taken by Henry Grant. This poor chap very smartly dressed surrounded by filthy brushes at the back of a sort of scruffy untidy canvas . . . and this poor chap looks half dead, he looks very bored, I can't see what this is supposed to show.

Teacher: He looks half dead; he looks bored. Do the rest of you feel that this is the attitude of mind this painter has? Boredom and half dead, whatever that means.

Boy: The position he has got in, it doesn't look as if he has done a hard day's work and flopped out; he looks as if he is trying to feel something to paint in the picture.

Boy: It is all very well to say boredom and half dead but for all you know this photograph could have been taken very early in the morning and he's suffering from the morning after the night before.

Teacher: Does it look as if he is suffering from the, that sort of hangover feeling? Or is it that as T said, that he is concentrating on his work, trying to feel something? What do you mean by feel something?

Boy: Well you know, if you want to paint a picture to know what colours, something like that and he wants to feel the picture to paint it properly.

Teacher: Does that then tell us something about his attitude towards his work by comparison with some of the other photographs that we have seen.

Boy: I think you have got to be a pretty dedicated person and if that's the case . . .

Boy: No I wouldn't say so. From this picture I would gather that he has been working because of the horrible mess on the table.

Boy: Yes, but he has got a nice suit on, he wouldn't be working like that.

Boy: Yes, but . . .

Boy: Yes, but why has he got it on.

Boy: . . . perhaps he is having a five-minute break. But he would not take it off for just a five-minute break.

Boy: Just to sit in a chair.

Teacher: Does it matter? Is it important?

Boy: Yes, we don't know you see.

Boy: He might be excited by his work, he might be tired, he might be just started.

Teacher: This is bringing out, is this not bringing out points about people and their work?

Boy: We have said all we can say about it and are just going round in circles.

Boy: If we look at this photograph closely we can determine things. To start off with the canvas on which the painting can be done (he might even have finished the painting for all we know) we cannot see; he has obviously been working because of the mess on the table; the pots are open, the paint brushes are still in the paint.

Boy: It doesn't necessarily mean he has been working that day. He could have been working the day before and he knocked off and didn't bother to clear up.

Teacher: Why is that important? Does that matter?

Boy: We are trying to assume what this fellow is trying to mean, what he is trying to put over. This chap Henry Grant is a good-spirited sort of fellow, but he is putting in very awkward sort of photographs.

Boy: It could be an important thing that he has been painting because say he has finished the painting, he could be looking at this large painting he has just done, the masterpiece of his life, and thinking 'God what a marvellous fellow I am', or it could be he is just standing at the canvas and thinking 'help what I am going to do? I've got to produce this painting and I can't get anything in it.'

Boy: I got this canvas, and I got the picture, and the person sitting down is someone who is posing for a picture which is being painted. He could be sort of posing in that position. That explains why he is sitting in a mucky place like that.

Boy: Now let's assume that he is the artist. No. 2008 is another artist which is a potter at work. He looks content with his work. He looks as if he is enjoying himself. He is creating something as I would imagine the artist on page 2010.

Teacher: You have brought up the point about contentment of work. There are jobs which provide contentment.

Boy: In fact there are two different sources. One you either enjoy your job and you are doing the job for enjoyment. Two you just work for the sake of getting money to support your wife and five kids.

Teacher: Is that contentment?

Boy: That is contentment, yes, because he is content in slogging away all week, or doing whatever job he is doing just to keep his family.

Teacher: Would you agree with him, that that is contentment?

Boy: Naturally, I think what he means by slogging all week is the same as my idea of people trying to get more money. Monied people nowadays represent paradise because with money you can buy almost everything to make paradise. For instance you could buy your own desert island, enough milk chocolate bars to last you for several years, all the birds you wanted and enough money. People I think sometimes tend to get a job with as much money as possible so after a while they can give up this job and go off to the desert island . . .

Boy: Picture 2007 is a school mistress at work. She is surrounded by young children she is obviously enjoying herself. She doesn't look bored, she looks very contented at her work. She must be a very patient woman.

Boy: You must remember that there are times of happiness and boredom in all jobs because for instance even in a factory job there is a time of happiness when you receive your pay packet.

Boy: Yes, but it is more than likely that you would look more happy when you are getting your pay packet than you would when you are not getting your pay packet.

Boy: But is it worth it just for that little bit of happiness?

Boy: I know but that's the point. If someone came along and took a photograph of this bloke smiling all over his mush, clutching his pay packet at that particular time, you'd think 'oh he looks very pleased with his job. He is a nice happy lad, he's all right. Let's get on with our other stuff.' But for all we know for the rest of the week he could have been slogging away very unhappy, very upset, and you wouldn't know anything about it, because this photograph was taken when he was getting his pay packet. (Fifth-year group discussion, from 'Visual material as evidence', mimeo, Humanities Curriculum Project.)

4. THREE TRANSCRIPTS ILLUSTRATING SOME COMMON TEACHER TALK STRATEGIES

Teacher: You get the white . . . what we call casein . . . that's er . . . protein . . . which is good for you . . . it'll help to build bones . . . and the white is mainly the casein and so it's not actually a solution . . . it's a suspension of very fine particles together with water and various other things which are dissolved in water . . .

Pupil 1: Sir, at my old school I shook my bottle of milk up and when I looked at it again all the side was covered with . . . er . . . like particles and . . . er . . . could they be the white particles in the milk . . .?

Pupil 2: Yes, and gradually they would sediment out, wouldn't they, to the bottom . . .?

Pupil 3: When milk goes very sour though it smells like cheese, doesn't it?

Pupil 4: Well, it is cheese, isn't it, if you leave it long enough?

Teacher: Anyway can we get on? . . . We'll leave a few questions for later.

Teacher: Now what do we mean by language?

Pupil 1: The alphabet.

Teacher: That's part of it . . . what else?

Pupil 2: How to speak.

Teacher: How to speak . . . yes . . . what else? . . . What else do you do with a language apart from speaking it?

Pupil 3: Pronounce it.

Teacher: Well that's part of speaking . . . What else?

Pupil 4: Learn to say it.

Teacher: Still the same thing . . . yes?

Pupil: Sir, you can tell the countries by the language they speak.

Teacher: Yes, but what else can we use a language for? We don't always speak a language . . . I don't always speak a language when I want to get something over to someone who is not in the same room . . . probably a long way away . . . I can't shout or use the telephone . . . What do I do?

Pupil: Write.

Teacher: I write . . . right, therefore it's the written word as well as the spoken word.

Teacher: How does the fish obtain the oxygen from the water? What happens . . ? Stephen?

Pupil: It allows the water to run over its gills and the . . . er . . . and extracts the oxygen.

Teacher: First of all think of it in stages, Stephen. Where does the water go first of all?

Pupil: Miss, it enters the mouth and then it passes over the gills taking out the oxygen. Then it comes out of the gills.

Teacher: Comes out of the back of the gill-cover.

(From *Language, the Learner and the School* by Douglas Barnes, James Britton, Harold Rosen and the LATE (Penguin, 1969).)

5. CAN THE STUDENTS SEE ANY WAYS IN WHICH ACTIVE PARTICIPATION IN DISCUSSION CAN BE ENCOURAGED?

You could make up two groups — one of people who talk, and one of them that are shy' (silent girl from a rural secondary modern school in the south of England).

Question: Can you think of any other way or situation in which it would be easier to talk or discuss?

Girl: Well, they put all the tables in a big, long table so we have to sit facing each other, but I think if they left the desks as they were we could talk to each other across the room, and that would be better . . . 'cos one of the other groups tried that . . . and they get a much better discussion (silent girl from a mixed, urban comprehensive school).

Girl: 'Starting off a discussion is the worst part, I think.

Question: And how do you get it going now?

Girl: 'Don't be scared to bring up your point of view — that's what I've found. I mean, if nobody's going

151

to say something, you might as well say something. They can't laugh at you for saying something, really.

Question: Do you feel you want to continue taking part in these kinds of discussions?

Boy: Yes, if there were more people who would talk sensibly.

Girl: I wonder what would happen if you put all the silent people together in a group?

Question: What do you think of that?

Boy: Well, I think they might talk if they were in a less talkative group, I suppose.

Boy: I think it's best to find out who the silent ones are first, and then next time we have a discussion, ask them to start it off.

Boy: They won't . . . We tried it . . . no one talked at all.

(From an interview with four dominant members from a fourth year Humanities group in a rural school, from Helen Simons, 'The silent pupil in discussion', mimeo, Humanities Curriculum Project Evaluation Unit.)

6. THE PHYSICAL ENVIRONMENT AND ITS CONSTRAINTS ON DISCUSSION AND THE ROLE OF THE TEACHER IN DISCUSSION

The physical environment in which a group meets, the behaviour of the teacher, and the expectations of the pupils are all very important. They are not more influential than in conventional teaching situations, but there they are familiar and accepted, so that people conform to them automatically. They are far less understood in groups. The first essential is that the participants should be face to face with each other, all members of the group being able to talk with each other. This means that the number cannot be many more than twelve people, and eight is probably the optimal number. Seating arrangements are important. Preferably the chairs should be in a rough circle, and they should be similar to each other, indicating that similarity of participation is expected. Teachers have been so well drilled by the classroom structure of chairs and desks that they have difficulty in emancipating themselves from spatial asymmetry; when in a group they tend to take the biggest or more comfortable chair, placed at a greater distance from its neighbours than separates any of the others, and at the head of a table if there is one. Perhaps they take books or notes with them, and in a hundred subtle ways emphasize that they have come to teach whereas the others have come to learn. All this, of course, is done with the collusion of the pupils, who indeed, try as hard as they can to stop the teacher doing otherwise, for they also feel more comfortable in the familiar hierarchical situation.

The teacher's role requires great self-discipline; he must get out of the habit of talking, and into the habit of listening. This is not at all easy, especially for teachers who have made a success of didactic teaching. A tally of the interventions made by each of the participants is a very good corrective and listening to a tape recording is even better. The teacher should aim to make fewer contributions than the students, and should try to make each as short as possible. The quality of his contribution also is important, and should set a model for others to follow. He should be spontaneous rather than heavily logical and rational, and not strive after grammatical perfection. Permit yourself to be stumbling in speech, don't insist that the others let you finish your sentence, and never, never interrupt anybody. Don't leap in to repair any silence; let others learn to take responsibility for keeping the party going. Be prepared for some expression of hostility on the part of the pupils who want you to behave in the old-fashioned authoritarian way. All this comes slowly with experience, and it comes more quickly if you can be in a group yourself discussing the equivalent of the sort of topics you might set your pupils. (From 'Learning to think in groups', in M. L. J. Abercrombie, *Anatomy of Judgement* (Hutchinson, 1960).)

7. PRACTICAL IMPLICATIONS OF INQUIRY-BASED LEARNING

Second, the teaching strategy will be inquiry-based. We take this to imply groups of pupils discussing issues in the light of evidence and under the guidance of the teacher. Distinctions may be drawn between instruction-based, discovery-based and inquiry-based teaching. Instruction-based teaching implies that the task in hand is the teacher's passing on to his pupils knowledge or skills of which he is master. In discovery-based teaching the teacher introduces his pupils into situations so selected or devised that they embody in implicit or hidden form principles or knowledge which he wishes them to learn. Thus, Cuisenaire rods embody numerical principles, and certain scientific 'experiments' used in educational settings reveal scientific principles. Instruction and discovery are appropriate in the classroom whenever the desirable outcome of teaching can be specified in some detail and is broadly the same for every pupil.

Where a curriculum area is in a divergent rather than in a convergent field, i.e. where there is no simple correct or incorrect outcome, but rather an emphasis on the individual responses and judgements of the students, the case for an inquiry-based approach is at its strongest. This is the situation in the humanities.

This basic strategy of classroom procedure can be argued, we maintain, from the nature of the content area. Considerations of professional ethics are also involved.

Each of the areas of study we have chosen involves highly controversial value judgements of a kind which divide opinion in our society, and this is bound to be so. It is just this controversial aspect of the work which offers the prospect of live significance; and conscientious teachers will quite properly feel diffidence in entering these areas unless their classroom strategy gives some assurance that the pupils will not have their horizons limited by their teacher's biases. Moreover, teachers are bound to find themselves working in areas of knowledge outside their own specialist qualifications and they ought to feel some reserve about playing an instructional role in this situation. A further consideration is that many of the subjects proposed for study may well be just those most likely to exacerbate the inter-generational and the inter-social class conflicts between teacher and pupil to which recent studies have drawn attention.

On all these grounds, it seems reasonable to assert that an inquiry-based strategy is demanded in the classroom when the school adopts a humanities curriculum as we have defined it. In short, inquiry is not simply a dispensable means to an end which could be reached by other routes.

The classroom strategy of inquiry is by no means new. Many of the ideas behind it can be seen in project work, for example. It is our view, however, that inquiry-based learning has seldom been entirely successful. Certainly, in the past, its adoption in the schools in response to fashion has sometimes led to a deterioration of quality. Teachers whose judgements were secure while they were working within an academic and instructional framework have suffered from the lack of supporting tradition when they moved over to a different style of teaching. The pattern of traditional academic teaching is so familiar that it is easy to forget the profound theoretical roots which lie beneath it.

Even the shift of role which is asked of a teacher as he moves from instruction to inquiry and discussion is likely to prove demanding. The teacher has to abandon his role as imparter of information and the dominant and didactic style which often goes with it. Instead he is asked to become the chairman of a committee of inquiry or a discussion group.

153

We have enough experience of student complaints about the conduct of seminars in higher education to be aware that the role of a rigorous, but patient and unobtrusive, critic is a difficult one for the instructor or lecturer to fill.

Given the inquiry base, and the difficulties it presents, we believe that the best chance of developing a core tradition of disciplined teaching lies in the exploration of the possibilities opened up by a type of discussion which is not so much an exchange of views as an interpretation of evidence, We start therefore from a model of the classroom situation in which the input of information comes not through the teacher, but through materials which demand critical interpretation. We hope that the close interpretation of evidence can strengthen and stiffen discussion so as to provide a group experience which is a firm centre for an inquiry-based approach. That established, we can explore the possibilities offered by individual and group investigations which feed into discussion, and various types of pupils' work which can develop out of it. (From Lawrence Stenhouse, 'The Humanities Curriculum Project', *Journal of Curriculum Studies*, 1(1) (November 1968).)

8. COMMUNICATION

Much of what I have to say in the following pages pivots on the inordinate capacity of a human being to learn more than one thing at a time. Although it is true that all the higher orders of animals can learn several things at a time, this capacity for polyphasic learning reaches unparalleled development in man. A child writing the word 'August' on the board, for example, is not only learning the word 'August' but also how to hold the chalk without making it squeak, how to write clearly, how to keep going even though the class is tittering at his slowness, how to appraise the glances of the children in order to know whether he is doing it right or wrong, etc. If the spelling, arithmetic or music

lesson were only what it appeared to be, the education of the American child would be much simpler; but it is all the things the child learns *along with* his subject matter that really constitute the drag on the educational process as it applies to the curriculum.

A classroom can be compared to a communications system, for certainly there is a flow of messages between teacher (transmitter) and pupils (receivers) and among the pupils; contacts are made and broken, messages can be sent at a certain rate of speed only, and so on. But there is another interesting characteristic of communications systems that is applicable to classrooms, and that is their inherent tendency to generate *noise*. *Noise*, in communications theory, applies to all those random fluctuations of the system that cannot be controlled. They are the sounds that are not part of the message: the peculiar quality communicated to the voice by the composition of the telephone circuit, the static on the radio, and so forth. In the classroom lesson on arithmetic, for example, such *noise* would range all the way from the competitiveness of the students, the quality of the teacher's voice ('I remember exactly how she sounded when she told me to sit down'), to the shuffling of the children's feet. The striking thing about the child is that along with his arithmetic — his 'messages about arithmetic' — he learns all the noise in the system also. It is this inability to avoid *learning the noise with the subject matter* that constitutes one of the greatest hazards for an organism so prone to polyphasic learning as man. It is this that brings it about that an objective observer cannot tell which is being learned in any lesson, the *noise* or the formal subject matter. But — and mark this well — it is *not* primarily the message (let us say, the arithmetic or the spelling) that constitutes the most important subject matter to be learned, but the noise! The most significant cultural learnings — primarily the cultural drives — are communicated as *noise*. (From *Culture against Man* by Jules Henry (Penguin, 1972).)

9. AT THE BLACKBOARD

Boris had trouble reducing 12/16 to the lowest terms, and could only get as far as 6/8. The teacher asked him quietly if that was as far as he could reduce it. She suggested he 'think'. Much heaving up and down and waving of hands by the other children, all frantic to correct him. Boris pretty unhappy, probably mentally paralysed. The teacher, quiet, patient, ignores the others and concentrates with look and voice on Boris. She says, 'Is there a bigger number than two you can divide into the two parts of the fraction?' After a minute or two, she becomes more urgent, but there is no response from Boris. She then turns to the class and says, 'Well, who can tell Boris what the number is?' A forest of hands appears, and the teacher calls Peggy. Peggy says that four may be divided into the numerator and the denominator.

Thus Boris's failure has made it possible for Peggy to succeed; his depression is the price of her exhilaration; his misery the occasion for her rejoicing. This is the standard condition of the American elementary school, and is why so many of us feel a contraction of the heart even if someone we never knew succeeds merely at garnering plankton in the Thames: because so often somebody's success has been bought at the cost of our failure. To a Zuni, Hopi or Dakota Indian, Peggy's performance would seem cruel beyond belief, for competition, the wringing of success from somebody's failure, is a form of torture foreign to those non-competitive redskins. Yet Peggy's action seems natural to us; and so it is. How else would you run our world? And since all but the brightest children have the constant experience that others succeed at their expense they cannot but develop an inherent tendency to hate — to hate the success of others, to hate others who are successful, and to be determined to prevent it. Along with this, naturally, goes the hope that others will fail. This hatred masquerades under the euphemistic name of 'envy'. (From *Culture against Man*, by Jules Henry (Penguin, 1972).)

10. PROBLEMS ABOUT THE CHICKEN'S EGG

Ten boys and girls of 11—12 years old are looking at a chicken's egg. The teacher, a female, has asked the children if they think the shape of the egg is a good one. The transcription is full of fragmented sections — for instance, this first section which is a mixture of pupil response and teacher interruption

Pupil: If it were square. Well in there it's got more in.

Teacher is interrupted by another pupil who says:

Did you get some paper Anne?

Teacher: Yes I gave it to John (another teacher in the class).
Pupil: It's more the shape of the egg — baby — if it's in a circle it would just have to turn round in a circle all the time.
Teacher: (laughs in light disbelief)
Pupil: No, it's because the chick's like that and not like that.
Pupil: Well — it's long shaped.
Pupil: It's got legs.
Pupil: Some people think the yellow is the chick but it's the blood forming on it . . .
Teacher: Well we'll cone on to that. I'm still a bit worried about the shape.
Pupil: (continuing his last statement) . . . no that's the food.
Pupil: So it won't roll around.

The teacher at this point takes the egg from the bench.

Teacher: You're right. They say it won't. It's short.

The teacher puts it on the bench and rolls it.

Teacher: Oh it's rolling about but it's meant to be a shape that's useful for keeping it in the nest.

Pupil: What about a square? (He starts to laugh knowing that what he has said is mischievous.)

Teacher: Have you ever seen a glass paperweight the shape of an egg?

Pupil: Yes.

Teacher: Well, that's because it's supposed to sit on the paper and also go round like that in preference to rolling. Anyway do you think it's a good idea to have this hard outside bit here?

Pupils: Yes, yes.

Pupil: So it protects the chick.

Pupils: And it throws the beak into its . . .

Teacher: Now if the chick's inside . . . All right, do you think this must be completely sealed up?

Pupils: Yes.

Pupil: Does it . . .

Pupil: Some people say that birds eat milk . . . eats these little stones.

Teacher: Oh I know what you are talking about, we'll talk about that in a minute. Now I'm thinking about if there's a chick living inside here . . .

Pupils: Yeah . . .

Teacher: . . . do you think that chicks wants to be surrounded by a very, very tough . . . where there's not a single hole?

Pupil: Yeah, for anything to get through.

Pupil: No, it's living, yeah, because it might be eating.

Teacher: Does that chick want anything in there, what sort of things does he want in there?

Pupil: Yellow yolk.

Teacher: He wants food, yes, but what else does he want.

Pupil: Air.

Teacher: Air, air, yes, only a little bit. Doesn't need too much but he wants air though doesn't he?

Pupil: Got to have some.

Pupil: Where do you get air from?

Teacher: Ah well, if you were to magnify this you would find that there's some little gaps going through, but just by looking at it, just like this, the gaps are so small we can't see them.

Pupil: Oh I get you, get it.

Teacher: All right, so air can get through. Anyway, let's have a crack inside.

Pupil: You could blow it, that would be better.

Teacher: Oh no, we want to see exactly what's happening on the inside. (She breaks the egg)

Pupils: Oh it's broke, yolk, yolk, yolk, you've got the yolk,

Teacher: Oh, I have the yolk.

Pupil: The yolk's broke.

Teacher: I need tweezers . . . there we are (Pupils laugh) . . . now somebody said that the yolk wasn't the chick.

Pupil: It is.

Pupil 1: That's why he causes that.

Pupil 2: Well it can't be yolk because that's what it eats.

Pupil 3: . . . little bit formed . . .

Pupil: Might be a cannibal . . . might eat the yolk . . . cannibal ate it.

Pupil: When we collect these . . .

Teacher: Let's see if I can pull the shell off and get a sort of white thing. Do you know when you pull the egg sometimes . . .

Pupils: Yes . . .

Teacher: . . . There's like a skin . . . you see that bit of skin there? . . .

Pupils: Yes.

Teacher: . . . flapping around in here so it looks as if there's a shell and inside the shell there's a sort of skin.

Pupil: Polythene bag.

Teacher: Yes, polythene bag. What do you think it wants a sort of polythene bag for?

Pupil: So if he gets any bangs.

Pupil: He wouldn't be able to breathe if it were a polythene bag.

Teacher: Now that's a point so the polythene must . . .

Pupils: . . . have holes in . . .

Teacher: . . . still have holes in so that, um, what do you get in . . .

Pupils: Air.

Teacher: . . . what's the special part of air?

Pupils: Oxygen.

Teacher: Have you heard of oxygen before?

Pupil: I said that.

Teacher: Oxygen's a thing that you want from the air.

Pupil: . . . just caved in (referring to the egg) . . . all runny isn't it?

Pupil: Drink it. Oh I drink it.

Teacher: Well let's go back . . . so the skin, we want the skin. The skin has got to let oxygen through to the chick, yes?

Pupils: Yes.

Teacher: So why do you think it's got a skin?

Pupil: We've got a skin.

Teacher: Think about this shell round here so that . . . so if we took this egg out of here and put it in the sun what would happen?

Pupil: It would dry up.

Teacher: Dry up . . . just an egg with no skin, but an egg with a shell round it with lots of holes . . .

Pupils: Dry, dry up, dry up again.

Teacher: But you know eggs don't dry up.

Pupil: Because they have plastic, little skins, whatever you call them.

Teacher: Yes, so what do you think the skin is there for?

Pupil: To stop it from drying up.

Teacher: So what's it keeping inside the egg?

Pupils: Food.

Teacher: Er, um . . .

Pupil: Is that why chicks are wet when they come out?

Pupil: Keeps it cool.

Teacher: . . . keeping the water in . . . that thing that's keeping it wet, water, keeping the water in, inside here. Anyhow, now let's have a look . . . see the yolk . . .

Pupils: Er . . . yuk . . . it's all flung out.

Teacher: . . . what's this called, what's the real name for this? We call it what?

Pupils: Yolk white.

Teacher: Right, yes, white yes.

Pupil: White.

Teacher: If you . . .

Pupil: (interrupting) can't break it.

Teacher: . . . seems it won't come out.

Pupil: Why is that all like that?

Teacher: Oh hang on, what's this (with mock surprise) look at the end there, that sort of flap at the top there.

Pupils: Skin, skin.

Teacher: You can see the skin . . . hold on, we want to leave it on just for a minute, you see that flap.

Pupil: Yes, it won't come out.

Teacher: There's a little space up there, isn't there?

Pupil: Is that where it goes?

Pupil: I mean, isn't that bulge the air?

Pupil: No it's the skin come away from the shell.

Teacher: It's come away from the shell. Does it often come away from the shell like that?

Pupil: Yeah.
Pupil: No.
Teacher: You think of that egg you had for breakfast, now sometimes you find a little . . .
Pupil: Yeah.
Teacher: . . . place like that so you usually find it. That's called the airspace and that's sort of an extra supply, so that's air, so it's got some air in there. Now can you see some white bits floating?
Pupils: Yeah.
Teacher: Can you see some white bits down here?
Pupils: Yeah.
Teacher: Let's see if there are any up the other end.
Pupil: That's the shell ain't it?
Teacher: Oh I can't see any at the other end. There's sort of white bits attached there.
Pupil: Oh that's what they are.
Teacher: They're called strands, yes. Can you see a strand there.
Pupil: Yeah, Oh something like that on the yolk ain't it?
Teacher: Yes, doesn't seem to look as if there's another thing to keep the yolk away from the white anyway. Anyway they are strands. What do you think it's there for?
Pupil: Feeding it
Teacher: Well wait a minute, let's decide where it is first, now that you've been saying all along that the yolk isn't the chick, how do you . . .
Pupil: No it's the food . . . a little bit forms on top of it.
Teacher: Right, so it's quite a small thing somewhere on the yolk isn't it? Have you ever heard this before. He's dead right actually.
Pupil: This woman told me that the blood comes on the top.
Teacher: What's that little red streak?

Pupil: . . . after it's been left for a long while . . .
Teacher: That's right.
Pupil: . . . in a warm place.
Teacher: That means you've got a little chick beginning to develop there. It hasn't got very far but the little red streak is him sitting on top there and he's spreading out his blood so that he can take in the food of the yolk.
Pupil: How can it form out of blood?
Teacher: Form what out of blood?
Pupil: Chick.
Teacher: Oh well what did we say a chick was going to be made up of at the very, very beginning, to make a chick we are going to have two things: a sperm and an egg . . .
Pupil: Yeah.
Teacher: So at the beginning there must have been a little sperm and a little egg on top here.
Pupil: Yeah.
Teacher: . . . develop and develop and is obviously going to start needing lots of food, the bigger and bigger he gets the more food he is going to want so he starts spreading . . .
Pupil: Food around.
Teacher: . . . blood so that er . . . (she makes a sucking sound to indicate sucking in food) . . . so he's sitting on the top there somewhere.
Pupil: There's a little black thing.
Teacher: No I don't think that's it — it's probably my mucky tweezers. Anyway, chick on top — yolk is his food and these little strands, these come out of one end and out the other. have you got any idea about those?
Pupil: So he doesn't want them inside.
Teacher: Something to do with wanting . . .

Pupil:	Hold it.
Teacher:	Yes that's right — to keep it in the middle.
Pupil:	If it was a fat chicken the strands might break.
Teacher:	No, it means whenever it rolls round the strands always manage to keep it in the middle so it doesn't get too near the edge where it might get banged. What do you think that all of this white is up the other end. What do you think it is all about?
Pupil:	To drink from.
Teacher:	Er, er, you've got an idea there you know.
Pupil:	Drink.
Pupil:	That's the food.
Teacher:	It's to keep the . . . drink.
Pupil:	Yeah, but it's queer ain't it — keep it from going dry.
Teacher:	That's it, yes, and also you can — anyhow this will be jolly difficult for the yolk to go crashing against the edge when there's all this mushy stuff in between.
Pupil:	Oh yeah.
Teacher:	That's it then . . . Now I think we've seen everything. Now let's tip it out.
Pupil:	Let's have a look at the yolk.
Teacher:	Oh that's bust hasn't it and I can't see the strand at the other end but usually there's a strand at the other end attaching it to the white part.
Pupil:	What's this?
Teacher:	The strand that's coming from the yolk and keeps it in the middle. Remember I said so . . . Let's talk about the very beginning inside the mother chick. Right.

APPENDIX 2. A photographic record of one lesson

Teacher: Berris Bowen, Middle school, small town in rural
    area
Class size: Thirty-six, mixed ability boys and girls
Group structure: friendship groups
Apparatus: newspapers brought in by the children, PVA,
    glue, sellotape.
Aim of the lesson: To see what strong structures the
    children could make.
Background: The children's own environment.
Brief to the children: Paper supplied, 'what strong structures
    can you make?' No other details.

As lesson progresses and tubes are made problems arise with fixing of tubes. Tubes have to be stuck with glue.

Still rolling tubes!

As problems arise some children attempt to work as a group designing the structure on paper first.

Putting tubes into each other to form long tubes.

Using plasticine, then putty to fix the structure on the floor.

Gently testing structures to see where support is needed.

Some children had difficulty rolling tubes of paper.

Beginnings of structures taking shape.

Use of triangular shapes.

Close co-operation and discussion between members of the groups.

One of the few occasions most children gathered round one structure — because they thought it was strong.

While I am talking with one group the rest of the class are working.

'Tell me about your structure'.

The group finished to their satisfaction and started writing about their structure.

One of the members of this group is the daughter of an architect!

Still rolling tubes!

'Let me try it — it feels quite strong.'

'Don't try it too hard just yet!'

'May I make this point?'

'More string.'

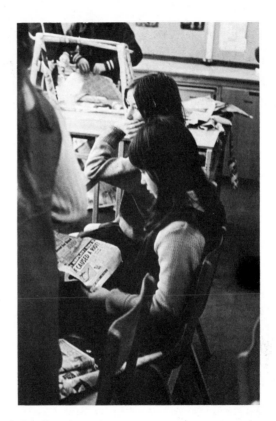

Reading the papers.

Still rolling tubes.

These links are difficult to cut.

'I wonder if I can cut this one.'

Conclusion of lesson. Discussion of structures.
'What shapes have we used?' All triangles.

After

'How can we test which is the strongest structure?'
Each group to press their structure until it collapses.

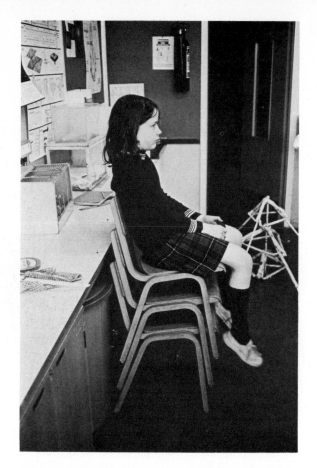

One small girl sits on three chairs to see.

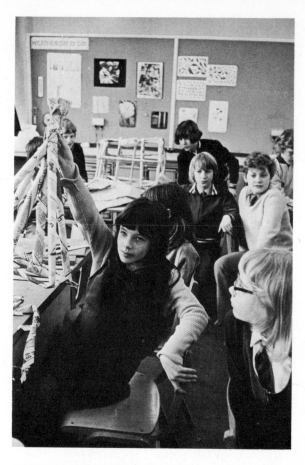

Holding up the structure for all to see before testing.

The test.

Two poorer boys academically telling the class about their structure and testing it.

'Who thought this was a strong structure?'

This one needs two hands.

Final vote on the winner and reasons.

Because this one was on the floor everyone gathered round to see it.

Clearing up.

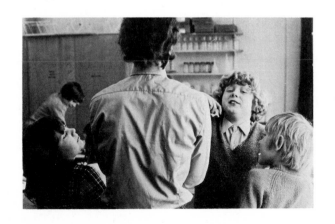

APPENDIX 3. Organizing a course-sample scheme

We have already described the context in which we worked at Chelsea and outlined the course structure. Few other colleges provide the kind of facilities, resources or overall context we had there, so what we have reported here may be read as an account of 'what might be done if . . .'. Those who do have a similar situation may wish to note our experience and pursue alternative lines; others may dismiss the possibility of using anything we have suggested because they feel constrained by time, money, staffing ratios, course structures or exam systems. We do not think it is necessary to pursue all the ideas we have suggested at one go. We have tried to describe the whole enterprise as a coherent whole because that is the way we need to justify it for ourselves. We do not however perceive what is written here as a total curriculum or as a total enterprise within the curriculum. Individual tutors, colleges and students must be free to take from it what they feel to be interesting and relevant to their needs. They must also feel responsibility for their own actions and not hold us responsible.

The course we ran had the following basic structure. It was part of a one-year PGCE course for science and mathematics graduates.

STUDY GROUP
Eight to twelve students meeting for a half day once a week.

AUTUMN TERM
First meeting during induction course. Introductions. We gave out observation guide and introduced the idea of mini-teaching.

First teaching practice (three weeks)
In the second week we did the mini-teaching exercise.

Return from teaching practice. Discussion of varieties of schools. of the schools they went to as kids compared to where they teach etc.

Communication games
(From one to three sessions.)
Looking at recordings from classrooms often with the teacher present (up to three sessions).
Film, *Space between Words — School* (BBC).

SPRING TERM
Second teaching practice (usually in same school as first).

During the second practice we attempted to record one lesson from each student, playing them back the recording as soon as possible. An idea we tried to develop but had only limited success with was to get students working in small groups in different schools. The idea was that they should visit each other, record each other's lessons and develop a group interest in studying their own teaching.

SUMMER TERM
Discussion on teaching practice (recorded).
Usually a focus on language and talk and on the social relationships of the classroom.
Use of teaching practice recordings.
Film (*'Who saw him die?'*)
Visits to schools, including the school the mini-teaching children came from.
Discussion using selected extracts.
This plan only roughly sums up what we did — we saw most of the students daily — some we were supervising through the specialist subject departments, others through their dissertations. There were few occasions when the pace dropped and we had to think hard of something to

do — usually the problem was the opposite one of selecting the most pressing issue.

Obviously in a three-year course the scheme might work out quite differently. Our feeling is that although, for us, each event and activity related closely to each of the others and formed a coherent and developing whole, there is no reason why any bit might be extracted and used independently.

Fundamentally what we are arguing for is a reorientation of courses away from a primary dependence on the published outcomes of theory and research. Instead we want the focus to be on the individual's experiences of teaching and learning. We see most available research as related more to the concerns of tutors than to the concerns of teachers. We would like actual research methods and processes to be taken up as part of courses more than their rationales or outcomes.

This shift is not an easy one to accomplish but we have tried to make our ideas accessible in a way that enables people to take bits and pieces to try out in ways they can themselves control. Our hope is that with growing confidence they will be able to reorientate their own courses.

APPENDIX 4. Useful additional material

Books

Jules Henry, *Culture Against Man* (Penguin, 1972).

Willard Waller, *The Sociology of Teaching* (Wiley, 1967). First published in 1932 it remains the classic text. The contents pages alone make stimulating reading.

Philip Jackson, *Life in Classrooms* (Holt, Rinehart and Winston, 1968). Chapters 1 and 5. These two chapters represent a starting point for a radical reappraisal of the relationship between teaching and research. If that wasn't the meaning you got from them when you read the book — read it again.

Louis Smith and William Geoffrey, *Complexities of an Urban Classroom* (Holt, Rinehart and Winston, 1968). A carefully documented account which reveals what the kind of research Philip Jackson describes as necessary might look like in practice.

James Britton, *Language and Learning* (Penguin 1972). The best contemporary resource book on ideas about the role of language in learning. Clear, accessible and exciting.

Robert Goldhammer, *Clinical Supervision. Special Methods for the Supervision of Teachers* (Holt, Rinehart and Winston, 1969). Chapter 6 — three case studies — extremely valuable for those involved in supervision or in micro/mini-teaching.

Bedtime reading

Michael Armstrong, *Reconstructing Knowledge — an Example* (Forum, spring 1975 vol. 17 No. 2 pp. 50—53).

Jennifer Dawson, *The Ha Ha* (Panther, 1966).

Caroline Glynn, *Don't Knock the Corners Off* (Pan, 1963).

Bel Kaufman, *Up the Down Staircase* (Pan Books, 1973).

A. S. Neill, *A Dominie's Log* (Herbert Jenkins, 1915).

Nicholas Otty, *Learner Teacher* (Penguin, 1972).

Muriel Spark, *The Prime of Miss Jean Brodie* (Penguin, 1965).

Films

Space Between Words — School (BBC TV). From:
    BBC Enterprises Film Hire.
    25 The Burroughs
    Hendon
    London NW4. Tel: 01 202 5342.

High School, film by Frederick Wiseman, distributed by The Other Cinema, Little Newport Street, London WC2.

Bibliography

AMIDON, E. A. and HUNTER, ELIZABETH(1966) *Improving teaching*. Holt, Rinehart and Winston.

ASHTON-WARNER, SYLVIA(1966) *Teacher*. Penguin.

BIDDLE, B. J. and ADAMS, R. S. (1970) *The Realities of the Classroom*. Holt, Rinehart and Winston.

BOYER, E. G. and SIMON, ANITA (1967, 1970) *Mirrors for Behaviour*, 14 vols. Research for Better Schools Incorporated, Philadelphia.

BROWN, R. and BELLUGI, U. (1964) 'Three processes in the child's acquisition of syntax'. *Harvard Educational Review*, 34.

FIANDER, ANN (1973) 'What does education achieve: a case study of a teacher and six pupils'. GCSE dissertation, Chelsea College.

FLANDERS, N. A. (1971) *Studying Teaching Behaviour*. Wiley.

FRAKE, C. (1969) 'The ethnographic study of cognitive systems' and 'Notes on queries in ethnography', both in S. A. Taylor (ed.), *Cognitive Anthropology*. Holt, Rinehart and Winston.

HANNAM, SMYTH and STEPHENSON(1971) *Young Teachers and Reluctant Learners*. Penguin.

HOLLAND, R. (1970) 'George Kelly: constructive innocent and reluctant existentialist', in D. Bannister (editor), *Perspectives in Personal Construct Theory*. Academic Press.

KELLY, G. An introduction (1968) to his ideas and their operationalization is in D. Bannister and J. M. M. Mair, *The Evaluation of Personal Constructs*. Academic Press.

KIRK, S. and Hopkin, N. (ed.) (1972) *CATS Manual*. Centre for Advanced Television Studies, 15 Prince of Wales Crescent, London NW1.

KOUNIN, J. S. (1970) *Discipline and Group Management in Classrooms*. Holt, Rinehart and Winston.

Man: a course of study (1970) *Evaluation strategies*. Education Development Center, Cambridge, Massachusetts.

MEDLEY, D. M. and MITZEL, H. E. (1963) 'Measuring classroom behaviour by systematic observation', in N. L. Gage *Handbook of Research on Teaching*, first edition. Rand McNally.

RESEARCH COMMITTEE OF THE INSTITUTE AND FACULTY OF EDUCATION (1967) . . . *And Softly Teach*. Achievements in Teaching No. 3. University of Newcastle-upon-Tyne.

SPINDLER, G. (ed.) (1970) *Being an Anthropologist: fieldwork in eleven cultures*. Holt Rinehart and Winston.

WITHALL, J. (1956) 'An objective measurement of a teacher's classroom interactions'. *Journal of Educational Psychology*, 47, pp. 203–12.

Index

Notes